Mastering Basic Math Skills

Games for Third through Fifth Grade

Bonnie Adama Britt

NATIONAL COUNCIL OF
TEACHERS OF MATHEMATICS

www.nctm.org/more4u
Access code: MSG14508

Library of Congress Cataloging-in-Publication Data

Britt, Bonnie Adama, author.
 Mastering basic math skills. Games for third through fifth grade / by Bonnie Adama Britt.
  pages cm
 ISBN 978-0-87353-758-2
 1. Games in mathematics education. 2. Mathematics—Study and teaching (Elementary)—Activity
programs. I. Title. II. Title: Games for third through fifth grade.
 QA20.G35B754 2014
 372.7'049—dc23
        2013034229

The National Council of Teachers of Mathematics is the public voice of mathematics education, supporting teachers to ensure equitable mathematics learning of the highest quality for all students through vision, leadership, professional development, and research.

Printed in the United States of America

I tried to teach my child with books.
He only gave me puzzled looks.
I tried to teach my child with words.
They passed him by, unheard.
In despair I turned aside.
"How will I teach my child?" I cried.
Into my hand he put the key . . .
"Come" he said, "and play with me."

Unknown

Table of Contents

Preface vii

Acknowledgments ix

About Math Games

Why Use Math Games? 1

Parents Using Math Games 3

Teachers Using Math Games 7

Using the Games 15

The Games

Simple Addition 19

Place Value 41

Multidigit Addition 59

Rounding Numbers 75

Subtraction 85

Multiplication 113

Division 149

Multiple Operations in One Game 165

Fractions 197

Decimals 219

Money 239

Integers 253

References 266

Preface

I have a confession to make. I was one of those kids who never considered using the words *math* and *fun* in the same sentence! I struggled to understand math; I certainly didn't consider myself to be successful at it; I can't remember ever enjoying a single moment of it (probably a mild understatement!), and I avoided it like the plague in college!

Then, suddenly, I was an elementary school teacher, and I had to teach math! Well, how hard could it be? I only had to teach up to third grade math. I had managed to memorize the multiplication facts. What about fractions? The thought of multiplying fractions terrified me. No, you don't have to multiply fractions in the third grade. Whew! I was pretty sure I could do this!

I quickly realized that I was teaching math the way it had been taught to me in elementary school. Even though I had been an elementary education major in college, there had been no classes on how children learn math and how it should be taught. (Unfortunately, I think the situation is only a little better today.)

Needless to say, I was uninspired and uninspiring. I wasn't an effective math teacher, and neither my students nor I were in any way captivated by, or fascinated with, math. I decided that this status quo was not acceptable. I didn't want to repeat the past. I wanted to be a good teacher, and I wanted my students to love math! I had heard that was possible, although you certainly couldn't prove it by me! I had a lot of math to learn and a long way to go before I could teach it well.

I began by spending an entire summer at a math institute for elementary school teachers at the University of California at Riverside. Math started to become understandable. It was definitely challenging, exciting, and, yes (gasp!), fun! Who knew? All right, that was all well and good, but I realized that the journey had only just begun. So, I began work on a Master of Arts in Elementary Education at California State University at San Bernardino. My particular emphasis was on brain-based learning—how children learn and what that means regarding how they should be taught. I packed two years of course work into just five years! That's what happens when you are teaching full-time and working on a master's degree.

I read everything I could get my hands on about how children learn math and how to teach math in engaging and effective ways. As I learned, I began to change the way I taught. One of the things I realized was how very important it is to listen to and learn from the children—they are great teachers!

Much changed in my math classroom. One of the learning tools I began to experiment with was math games. As I watched the students play, I quickly realized that games were a wonderful, useful teaching tool.

In the years since I retired, I have worked in elementary schools all over southern California helping teachers, parents, students, administrators, and after-school child-care workers use math games to support their children in learning and practicing math concepts and skills. Their enthusiasm for these games as a teaching tool encouraged me to compile them, including their education rationales and some pointers I have picked up from playing the games with children.

The games in this book will provide children with—

- engaging opportunities to discover math concepts;
- stimulating math reinforcement; and
- the chance to discover that math can be fun and nonthreatening.

For parents and teachers, the games offer another effective and engaging way to help their children.

The best part is that parents, teachers, and children will enjoy playing the games in this book. So, get everyone together and start playing! Have fun!

More4U

Many of the games in this book use materials such as cards, number lines, recording sheets, and game boards. These can be found for downloading and printing on NCTM's More4U online resource. Simply go to www.nctm.org/more4U and enter the access code that is on the title page of this book.

Acknowledgments

After many years in the elementary classroom, I can say without any doubt that my students taught me more about how to teach than anyone else. I had no idea that was going to happen when I stepped into the classroom on the first morning of my teaching career. After all, I was the teacher and they were the learners. As it turned out, we were all learners.

So, thank you to Marcie (a second grader), who taught me that she was just as capable of answering a question as I was. Thank you to Brandon (a first grader), who pointed out five different and perfectly legitimate ways to solve an addition challenge. Thanks to the entire third grade who became so excited about solving a multiplication challenge that I couldn't get a word in edgewise. And that was as it should have been!

Thanks to Betty and John Clemens, my mathematics and writing mentors, who took a great deal of their precious time to question me, listen to me, read what I wrote, and nudge me in the right direction.

I will forever be grateful for my good friend, teaching partner, and fellow learner Carolyn Oleson.

Nelson Togerson was the very best principal a teacher could have. He knew how children learned and understood how they should be taught. Thanks, Nelson, for all you did to help me become a better teacher.

I will be forever grateful to Myrna Jacobs, the publications manager at NCTM. She knows that using games is an effective way to engage children in mathematics. Thank you, Myrna, for finding me and giving me this exciting challenge and opportunity.

Thanks to my excellent editor, Maryanne Bannon, for her expertise and patience.

And last, but definitely not least, thanks to my husband, Rex, for new beginnings, wonderful surprises, warm love, a constructive critical eye, insightful questions, and ongoing support and encouragement. He's a good cook, too!

Why Use Math Games?

There are some who wrongly think that teaching math games to children is a waste of valuable educational time. After years of teaching math to children and using games, I am convinced that math games are an immensely helpful resource for parents and teachers who want to make sure that their children develop and practice some of the skills they will need to become proficient with math in school and in life.

Third through fifth graders may seem mature and grown-up at times, but they still respond very well when learning is turned into a game. **The benefits of using math games with children are many:**

1. Games create a context for developing and supporting children's mathematical understanding and reasoning. They—

   - help children learn important mathematical skills and processes with understanding. That is, children do not just memorize rules but gain true knowledge of the concepts and processes. Understanding develops through interaction with materials, peers, parents, and teachers in settings where children have opportunities to discover and use number relationships;

   - require a variety of problem-solving skills. They help students develop the ability to think critically and solve problems. While playing a game, children eagerly make and test hypotheses, create strategies, think and plan ahead, and organize information;

   - are particularly effective in helping children make sense of how numbers work;

   - encourage strategic thinking. As children play math games, they develop mental strategies to compete successfully, understand the objectives, evaluate their own (and their opponents') strengths and weaknesses, learn routine procedures and probabilities, keep track of what is going on, and make short- and long-range plans; and

   - provoke children into debating, explaining, and thinking. Children learn from discussing, sharing, and reflecting throughout game sessions. The interaction required by games improves their ability to communicate and use mathematical language.

2. Through playing and analyzing games, children gain computational fluency.

   Math is like a ladder. If you miss a step, sometimes you can't go on. Elementary school provides a crucial window of opportunity for students to master certain skills in math. Students who haven't grasped certain mathematical concepts and skills by the end of elementary school are more likely to have problems in middle school, high school, and beyond.

   Games are an effective and engaging way to help children in third through fifth grade achieve mastery of basic facts. This means that children are able to give a quick response (in three seconds or less) without resorting to an inefficient computational strategy such as counting. Computational fluency plays a key role in helping children successfully work with higher-level math problems.

3. Games motivate children.

   Math games are inherently interesting, and because they are stimulating, intriguing, challenging, and fun, games motivate children to work at a task over and over again. Peggy Kaye (1987, p. 236), in her book *Games for Math*, put it perfectly when she said, "Games put children in exactly the right frame of mind for learning difficult things. Children relax when they play—and they concentrate. They don't mind repeating certain facts or procedures over and over, if repetition is part of the game. Children throw themselves into playing games the way they never throw themselves into filling out workbook pages. And games can, if you select the right ones, help children learn almost everything they need to master in elementary math."

4. Math games encourage parent involvement.

Games offer an effective and pleasant way for parents to help their children learn math by doing one of the things kids love—playing games. Parents appreciate the fact that there's no nagging or pressuring when a math game is proposed.

5. Games offer many opportunities for parents and teachers to discover their children's strengths and weaknesses.

Parents and teachers who observe and interact with their children while playing math games can discover a great deal about what they know and can do in math. Games provide feedback so that parents, teachers, and the children know what they have done well and what they need to practice.

6. Math games promote confidence and positive attitudes toward math.

They help children master not only mathematical skills, principles, and concepts but also to appreciate and enjoy math. Math games almost always motivate, excite, and challenge children.

7. Games meet the needs of diverse learners.

Because math games require active involvement, use concrete objects (sometimes called manipulatives by elementary teachers), and are hands-on, they offer multisensory support and are ideal for all learners. Games reinforce and sharpen math skills and concepts for children who are already good at math, and they stimulate, strengthen, and empower children who need extra help. Games cut across ages and genders. Players of widely varying abilities can have fun playing and learning together.

8. Math games teach life skills.

On the social level, game playing can help children learn to work cooperatively, give and take praise and criticism, instruct others, and accept success and failure in the presence of peers. In the process of playing a game, children may develop initiative, interest, curiosity, resourcefulness, independence, and responsibility. Plus, as children play, they further their development of hand-eye coordination, concentration levels, visual discrimination, and memory.

To sum up, math games—

- make children more open to learning;

- motivate them to keep practicing new skills;

- help children remember what they learn; and

- teach or reinforce many of the skills that a formal curriculum teaches, plus an element that math lessons sometimes unwisely leave out—having fun with math—and developing the skill of thinking hard and learning to enjoy it.

Parents Using Math Games

It's common knowledge that children whose parents read to them (even in third through fifth grade) have a tremendous advantage in school. But did you know that you can also help your child learn mathematics at home? Research by Greg J. Duncan and Amy Claessens (2007, 1428–46) shows that early math skills may very well be a better predictor of academic success than reading ability.

As my teaching career progressed, I frequently saw that children no longer memorized their addition facts or multiplication tables. With the math curriculum as extensive as it is, teachers cannot afford to take the time to ensure that all students know all the basic facts (sad, but true). Parents are partners in the process, and you can assure your children greater opportunities to succeed in math if you support reviewing the basics at home. Games fit the bill wonderfully!

Math games for children and families are the perfect way to reinforce and extend the skills children learn at school. They are one of the most effective ways that parents can develop their child's math skills without lecturing or applying pressure. When studying math, there's an element of repetition that's an important part of learning new concepts and developing automatic recall of math facts. Number facts (remember those times tables?) can be boring and tedious to learn and practice. A game can generate an enormous amount of practice—practice that does not have kids complaining about how much work they have to do. What better way to master number facts than by playing an interesting game?

Helping your child get better at math doesn't have to be difficult, painful, or scary. Don't be fooled—just because games are fun doesn't mean they are frivolous. We tend to think that when children are playing, they aren't learning and vice versa. But children do learn through play, and having fun can even help them learn more effectively.

In the process of playing a game, your child can develop initiative, interest, curiosity, resourcefulness, independence, and responsibility. It's doubtful that would happen with a problem-packed worksheet, workbook page, or flash cards.

As you join your child in these games, you will begin to perceive your child's strengths and weaknesses in math and know what he or she will need to practice. Any game can be changed to meet the needs of your child. Don't hesitate to go back to a game if you know your child needs to practice a particular skill.

Resources for Parents

The National PTA (http://www.pta.org) has provided *Parents' Guides for Student Success* at every grade level. These guides are based on the new Common Core State Standards, and provide an overview of the key skills your child should learn by the end of their present grade in language arts and mathematics. The Internet links to specific grade level content are provided in the References section on page 266.

Many of the games use special materials such as cards, game boards, and recording sheets. You can download them for printing by visiting NCTM's online resource at www.nctm.org/more4u. The access code can be found on the title page of this book.

Everyone can have fun

Your family will have fun together, too. Not so long ago, I had a mother tell me that her entire family (two parents and three children) had an enjoyable evening playing a particular math game. After the children went to bed, the parents continued to play!

Remember that card games are *games* (that is, they should be fun!). If pleasure is not connected to the game, children will be unwilling to play, and little learning will take place. Games are effective as teaching aids only as long as they are entertaining, and parents and children enjoy playing them together. You are investing time in something that can bring hours of pleasurable interaction—and learning math is an immense fringe benefit!

As the Internet continues to play a larger role in education, a growing number of online sites host free math games, most of which are challenging, exciting, fun, and age appropriate. That's all well and good, but above all else, children crave time with their parents. Because learning is a social process, children learn best through enjoyable games and activities that involve interaction with other people.

Indulge your children with your undivided attention, and play a math game. A price cannot be put on the quality of the time you will have spent with them. They will have fun learning, and they will remember those times with greater fondness than the hours they spent playing educational computer games.

Communicating

When playing math games with your children, your primary responsibility is to be enthusiastic and eager to play. Your second responsibility is to ask your children questions—questions that will encourage them to think and to verbalize what they are doing and why.

While playing a game, children don't always know what to do next. Here are a few good questions to help them begin to help themselves and not to rely on you, the parent, to give them the answer. As parents, we need to ask our children good questions to promote the kind of thinking they require to give good answers. Questions encourage reflection and help children make mathematical connections. Ask your children, "What can you do to help yourself?"

- Use counters, such as beans, paper clips, pennies, and so on, to figure it out?
- Draw a picture or diagram?
- Start with something you already know?

> When a child is faced with a new situation, connecting it to something he or she already knows is often helpful. For example, when your child is learning the multiplication facts for 6, you can ask, "If you know that 5 times 6 equals 30, how can that help you figure out what 6 times 6 equals?"

Be curious about how your child solves problems. Ask questions to understand his or her thinking. Here are a few more great questions to ask when playing a game:

- What card do you need?

- Which cards would not be helpful?
- Can you prove to me that a _____ is what you need?
- Why do you think that?
- How did you know to try that strategy?
- How do you know you have the right answer?
- Will this work with every number? Every similar situation?
- When will this strategy not work? Can you give me an example?
- What did you notice while playing the game?

> "Convince me that you are right" or "prove it" are not challenges, but are requests that can be used with children to encourage them to think more deeply and articulate the concepts they are using. At first, children find it difficult to respond, but the more they explain what they are thinking, the more competent they become.

When I demonstrate how to play a game, or I play a game with a child, I often think out loud, "Hmm, if I use a sixty-five, it will get me closer to one hundred than if I used a fifty-six." Children then "hear" what I am thinking, which helps them understand why I decided to play as I did. Perhaps it was a strategy that had not occurred to them.

Recording sheets

Many of the games include recording sheets. Writing down the problems and their solutions while playing a math game can be helpful to your child—and you. You will be able to note any strengths or weaknesses over a period of time and to see the growth and development of your child's math abilities, and your child can feel a sense of accomplishment when looking at the completed math work. When you begin a game with a recording sheet, have your child put the date at the top for easier comparisons later on.

Calculators

The calculator can be a valuable tool if a child understands the basic mathematical ideas, concepts, and meanings of numbers, counting, and operations (addition, subtraction, multiplication, and division). Each child should learn to solve problems by using mental and written calculations as well as a calculator. Even young children can use calculators to focus on the ideas behind computation rather than just on the act of calculating.

Use your judgment as to whether calculators will speed up or defeat the purpose of the game. If a calculator eliminates the thought process, it's not appropriate for that situation.

You can play math games anytime, anywhere

Wherever you go, you can carry a small zip-tight plastic bag containing a deck of cards, two dice, a small notebook (for keeping scores), and a pencil. Games can be played while traveling in the car or on an airplane, or waiting for—

- the car to be serviced;
- your order to arrive in a restaurant;
- the movie to start; and
- appointments at the doctor's or dentist's office.

Be assured that what you do to encourage your child's success in mathematics matters. Nothing affects the academic outcome for a child as much as the involvement of a parent.

Math games aren't just prescriptions for children struggling with math or needing a little more practice or looking for something to do. Pick a math game that sounds like fun. Grab a deck of cards or some dice, and invite your child to play for fifteen minutes. That's it! It's a quick and easy way to make a huge difference in your child's math abilities. Your child will get better at math, become more confident, and want to learn—and play—even more.

Teachers Using Math Games

Game playing hasn't been a traditional part of the math classroom. If a teacher did use a game, it was played in the last ten minutes on Friday or as a rainy-day recess activity. Occasionally, a teacher might use a math game in a small-group learning center or as a reward for finishing work. Games were considered to be frivolous and a waste of valuable time. This idea is quickly changing.

Teachers and administrators are beginning to realize that using games as part of math instruction provides many benefits. Math games—

- reinforce mathematical objectives and meet many of the third through fifth grade Common Core State Standards for Mathematics;
- are easily linked to and can supplement any mathematics textbook;
- are repeatable (reuse often and sustain interest and engagement);
- can be open-ended, allowing for multiple approaches;
- are easy to prepare;
- increase curiosity and motivation;
- establish a sense of community among the students;
- create a student-centered learning environment;
- reduce anxiety in the mathematics classroom;
- allow for cooperative learning opportunities;
- inherently differentiate learning;
- build strategy and reasoning skills;
- engage individual learners simultaneously;
- lead students to talk about mathematics; and
- compel players to work mentally.

Planning games for the classroom

Once students have been introduced to a new math concept and they have begun to understand it, they need to practice it. That's when games become appropriate and can enhance the learning experience.

When planning a game for the classroom, there are four simple steps to follow:

1. Make sure that you play the game with someone (spouse, your own kids, in grade-level teams) to gain familiarity with its rules and subtleties. Determine whether the rules need to be modified to meet the needs of your students.

2. Consider how you will teach the game to your class:

- You can play the game against the whole class.
- Two students could demonstrate while you explain.
- One student can play the game with you.

3. As you demonstrate how a game is played, think out loud so the children understand the strategy you might be using, for example, "I need to get as close to 1,000 as I can. If I use 535, I'll be closer to 1,000 than if I use 355."

4. Allow enough time to demonstrate the game or to remind the students how it is played and to let them settle in and play the game. (Fifteen minutes probably won't be adequate.) Remember that playing a game for the first time requires a period of learning and clarification. As students become more familiar with the game, they will spend less time checking the rules and more time exploring mathematical ideas and developing strategies.

Many of the games in this book feature game boards, recording sheets, or cards. These materials are available for downloading and printing at NCTM's More4U online resource center. Simply go to www.nctm.org/more4u and enter the access code that is on the title page of this book.

Helpful tips when using math games

- **To learn a game, pair students who are similar but not quite equal in their math understanding**. Be very deliberate about pairing students or forming small groups who will be playing the game on their own. Once children know a game, partner children at equal skill levels. Partnering students of dissimilar skill levels may sound like a good idea, but one of them is often very quickly bored, and the other may just give up. In addition, some students often think intuitively and cannot always explain the why or how of what they did. If a pair of children cannot explain their thinking to each other, then they cannot learn from each other.

- **Use games for specific purposes, not as time fillers**. Know what mathematical objective and Common Core standard will be met by playing the game.

- **Play the games repeatedly**. The only exception to this rule is a game that is too easy for everyone. However, through the years, I have discovered that games I thought might be too easy were often a challenge. Children do not begin to build strategies, plan ahead, or problem solve unless they have played a game several times.

- **Don't hesitate to go back to a skill and play a game if you know the students need to practice it**, even if the text has taken you on to something else.

- **Because you cannot be everywhere at once, players need to keep each other accountable.** I have students initial the other player's work if it is correct before they can take their turn. If it is not correct, players return the recording sheets to their partners and kindly suggest that they recalculate. To keep all players engaged, make sure students are taking turns, paying attention to the game, and checking their partner's work.

- **No multiplication "cheat" sheets allowed!** One day my third graders were playing a multiplication game. Some of them were still struggling with the memorization of the multiplication facts, so I decided to give them a multiplication cheat sheet. Big mistake! Every single student stopped thinking and just looked at the multiplication grid to find the answer. Not what I wanted!

- **Use your judgment as to whether calculators will speed up the game or defeat its purpose**. Calculators can be quite helpful for settling questions about answers, executing complex calculations, or keeping track of players' cumulative scores. If a calculator eliminates the thought process, it's not appropriate for that situation.

- **Recording the problems solved while playing a math game can leave a mathematical trail that is of great value to children, teachers, and parents**. Many of the games include recording sheets. Children can feel a sense of accomplishment as they look back at all the math work they have done; teachers can use the records for assessment; and parents will appreciate this "evidence" that their children are actually doing mathematics and not just "playing games."

- **Make sure all students are doing their own calculating and keeping their own scores**. Every once in a while I have discovered that one person on the team is keeping all the scores. In that case, only that one person is thinking and doing the math.

- **All the games can be transformed into ones where the high scorer is not the winner or into noncompetitive activities**. Most of the games in this book have been designed as competitive matches where the high scorer wins. One of the ways to reverse this is to have one of the players roll a die. If the number rolled is an even number, the player with the greatest answer or score is the winner. If the number rolled is an odd number, the player with the least answer or score is the winner. Many of the games can be played in such a way that players keep track of their own scores over a period of days and try to improve their previous day's score. Children can enjoy keeping graphs of this information themselves.

- **Have fun together**. If pleasure is not connected to the game, children will be unwilling to play and little learning will take place.

- **Sending a letter to parents that tells them how and why math games will be used in your classroom is a good idea**. It can allay any doubts that may arise when their children come home describing how they "played games during math today!"

Math games and teacher responsibilities

Assessment

Good games evaluate children's progress. Children's thinking often becomes apparent through the actions and decisions they make during a game. Assessment is the process of drawing reasonable inferences about what a student knows by evaluating what they say and do while playing the game. Games provide feedback so that both teachers and the children know what they have done well and what they need to practice.

Once a game is fairly familiar to children, move from group to group, listening and questioning. Make dated anecdotal records on which game is being played, what skill or concept is being practiced, and how each child is progressing. Not only does this help in assessing the children's strengths and weaknesses but it also allows you to differentiate instruction.

The recording sheets that children produce while playing games can be placed in assessment portfolios, creating a paper trail as evidence of mathematical development that can be of great value to children, teachers, and parents. When beginning a game with a recording sheet, children should put their names and the date at the top of the paper.

Games provide children with a powerful way of assessing their own mathematical abilities. The immediate feedback children receive from their peers while playing games can help them evaluate their own understanding of mathematical concepts and revise inefficient, inadequate, or erroneous ones.

Communication

While the students are playing the game, you should be moving from group to group listening to their conversations, asking questions, and insisting on high-quality communications among students. You should be modeling to the students the kind of questions you expect them to ask each other by your own probing questions:

- What card do you need?
- Which cards would not be helpful?
- Can you prove to me that a _____ is what you need.
- Why do you think that?
- How did you know to try that strategy?
- Will this work with every number? Every similar situation?
- When will this strategy not work? Can you give an example?
- Who has a different strategy?
- How is your answer the same as or different from _____ (another student)?
- Can you repeat your classmate's ideas in your own words?
- Do you agree or disagree with your classmate's idea? Why?

> "Convince me that you are right" or "prove it" are not challenges, but requests that can be used with children at any time. At first, children find it difficult to respond, but the more they explain what they are thinking, the more competent they become.

Too often players are willing to give their partners the answer, unwittingly sabotaging them and making it possible for some players to do no thinking whatsoever. Not good! Children need to be encouraged to help each other by asking questions. Every time you ask a question, you are demonstrating the kind of questions they should be asking each other:

- What can you do to help yourself?
- Could you use manipulatives to figure it out?
- Could you draw a picture?
- Can you start with something you already know?

> When a child is faced with a new situation, connecting it to something he or she already knows is often helpful. For example, when a child is learning the multiplication facts for 8, you can ask, "If you know that eight times six equals forty-eight, how can that help you figure out what eight times seven equals?"

I know that it is challenging not to give a child an answer. However, when you give a child the answer, who is solving the problem? Who is doing the thinking? Ask questions that will prompt them to think. Good questions promote reflection and help children make mathematical connections.

Differentiating instruction

It doesn't take long for most teachers to discover that their classrooms are filled with a cross section of students with varying abilities, learning styles, learning disabilities, and facilities with the English language.

Consider the complexity of games and the thinking skills involved, and adjust the games to encourage thought at various levels if necessary. After you have done some initial assessment, you may find that some students need to keep playing the game at its simplest level, while others need to move on to the variation, which is usually a more complex version of the game, or on to another game. Games in this book are arranged from the simplest to the more complex.

Classroom management

After years of playing math games with children from kindergarten through sixth grade, I have discovered that a tough love policy (that is, no second chances) works best. I explain the game and the rules (for example, no throwing of materials, no arguing, and so forth). If a student breaks a rule, that student is immediately out of the game and must complete a worksheet or workbook page. As that is not nearly as much fun as playing a game, discipline is immediately under control—most children will behave appropriately so they can play the game.

Here are a few suggestions I have found to work well:

- **Learning and understanding mathematics depends on communication (listening *and* talking)**. Many people think that a quiet room is one in which learning is taking place. I definitely disagree with that theory! When children are playing games in cooperative groups, they need to be able to talk with each other. These conversations can be very constructive if children take responsibility to make sure that all players in a game understand the operations, concepts, and facts being used within the game. Sharing a variety of strategies with each other leads to fluency with numbers and helps everyone see different ways to play. The bottom line: Teach each other and learn from each other.

- **Never sit down to play a game with an unpaired student**. If you do so, you have immediately lost control of what is going on while the children are playing the game, and you have no opportunity to listen, ask questions, or do assessments. Instead, make a group of three to play the game.

- **Play on the floor. This will help with discipline and noise level, and materials will not get mixed up**. Spread out so each team has its own space. (If playing on the floor is simply not an option, be sure to separate the groups as best as you can.) Partners need to interact with each other, but do not need to talk to others around them, which is what happens when they play at their desks. I've found that once children of any age know this rule, they do not complain. They want to play.

- Because they are playing on the floor, **it helps if each student has a clipboard** for recording sheets, keeping their own scores, or drawing a picture or diagram.

- **One thing I model for every single game, even at the fifth grade level, is how to decide who goes first** (paper-rock-scissors, highest or lowest number on the die, birth date, and so forth). If play order is not absolutely clear, some children will spend the entire game time arguing about who goes first.

- **Keep the number of players between two and four, so that turns come around quickly.** It is very helpful to pair two children against two children. That way they can discuss possible strategies with each other. Two brains are almost always better than one!

- **The first time your students play a math game, I guarantee you will wonder why you ever thought this would be a good idea!** Some level of chaos will reign. Don't worry—move from group to group quickly, putting out the fires. Don't forget the tough love. The second time they play the game, it will be much better, and the third time it will be great!

- **Never allow children to insult another player.** They may disagree with answers and ideas, but not people.

- **When using dice, give each team a large, heavy-duty paper plate on which to roll the dice.** Not only does this muffle the sound but it acts as a boundary for the dice. If the dice do not stay in the paper plate, that player loses a turn (another example of tough love). Every classroom has one or more of the how-far-I-can-throw-these-dice experimenters!

After the game

In order for students to learn from games, there are several tasks the teacher should keep in mind: Help the children focus on specific number concepts; ask them what strategies they are using; and encourage them to talk about their discoveries. Talking about the mathematics they are doing gives students the chance to clarify their thinking.

Always bring the children together to discuss what happened when they played the game. Interaction with each other helps children verbalize their thoughts, get feedback for their thinking, and hear other points of view. While you were watching them play the game, you may have noticed that some of them were using strategies that are worth sharing with the entire class. Realizing that there are different ways to approach a problem or to strategize about a process broadens learning opportunities. Students learn from one another as well as from their teachers.

Make notes on a clean copy of the game—what went well, what needed to be changed, and so forth. Put it with the math unit you are presenting; then next year, when you're ready to play, you won't have to reinvent that wheel.

Math games as homework

Math games for homework are not only the perfect way to reinforce and extend the skills children learn at school but they also encourage parents' involvement in their child's development. I have found that sending home a game already learned in class as homework for children to play with their parents is useful and welcomed by most parents. It helps give parents a sense of what can be learned from math games that are not based on workbooks or worksheets.

Every Friday I sent home a game with the students. (Each year, with the first game, I also sent a deck of ten-frame cards and two dice that were to be kept in a safe place because they would be needed throughout the school year.) My initial letter to parents included these points:

- Talk to each other while playing the games. Ask your child questions: "How can you figure out the answer?" "What card do you need?" "Which cards would not be helpful?" "Can you prove to me that a ____ is what you need?" or "Convince me that ____ is the right answer." Children learn from talking, sharing, and reflecting throughout game times.

- Give your child opportunities to change the games. The rules and instructions for all games are meant to be flexible. Allow your child to think of ways to change the equipment or rules. Encourage him or her to make a game easier or harder or to invent new games.

- Play the games many times over the next week. Children begin to build and practice strategies (for example, planning their moves in advance) only when the game is repeated often. Playing it just once or twice is not very helpful, unless the game is too easy for your child. If it's too easy or too hard, change it.

- Have fun together. If pleasure is not connected to the game, children will be unwilling to play, and little learning will take place.

A response form was included with every game, and it was the only thing due back the next Friday.

Parent Response to the Game

- What did you think of this game? Did you like it? Why or why not?
- Was this game too easy, too hard, or just right? How did you change it to meet the needs of your child?
- What do you think your child learned from playing this game?
- What did *you* learn about your child while playing this game? What are your child's strengths? What does your child need to practice?

Many parents took the form very seriously, and I learned a great deal about the children's interests, strong points, and weaknesses.

I quickly discovered that if I did not respond to the completed parent form, the parents stopped returning them. They mistakenly assumed that I did not care. So, I began writing brief notes on the completed forms asking questions or making statements. Often it was just a "Thank you" or "This was helpful to me!!" returned to the parents on the following Monday.

Evaluating math games

The National Council of Teachers of Mathematics believes that games can be effective tools for helping children understand math concepts and for practicing needed math skills. In terms of evaluating games for use with children, it states on its website (nctm.org):

> While we may jump at the opportunity to use math games as a way to engage today's learners, we must still be careful in evaluating them as effective means for teaching and learning. Some questions that might help you determine the value of a math game follow:

- Is there variety in the mathematical tasks? If you play the same game over, will you be asked different questions? Are there different pathways to the end?

- Are there opportunities to develop strategy while engaging in NCTM's Process Standards—problem solving, reasoning and proof, communication, connections, and representation?

- Is there a combination of chance and choice in the game? That is, are there both a random component (rolling a dice, drawing a card) and an opportunity to make a decision?

- Is the competition positive and nonthreatening?

- Is there embedded scaffolding? If a player gets stuck, are there hints?

- Are there suggestions to integrate the game into the classroom? Are there follow-up questions for teachers? Is there a way for teachers to track student progress?

- Is the length of play appropriate for classroom use?

- Was the math situated in a meaningful context? Does the game promote deeper understanding of mathematical concepts that is meaningful to the student?

- Do the students feel empowered and in control? In other words, do decisions have clear outcomes?

- Was clear feedback provided during each turn? Was the computation of scoring clear?

- Does the game encourage social play? The three Cs of game playing are competition, collaboration, and communication. Even single-player games can spark rich discussions of strategy. ((NCTM n.d.)

A few final words

Almost every elementary school teacher struggles to find productive ways to encourage students to understand and master basic math concepts and facts. Math games meet the varied needs of learners, offer opportunities to differentiate instruction, and are effective, motivational, and engaging.

Whether you're a new teacher, a teacher new to teaching math at a different grade level, or a veteran teacher looking for a fresh perspective, I would encourage you to give math games a try. Games engage children and enhance their math learning.

Using the Games

Each game gives children practice with a particular math concept or skill, or a few related concepts and skills, so they can give all their attention to mastering those one or two items. The more children play, the more they will learn and improve. Some concepts and skills are repeated in two or more games. Play the ones you like the best.

The games

The games under each heading progress from the simplest to the more advanced. Many of the games have variations that can make the game different or more complex.

Under the title of each game, grade levels and correlating Common Core State Standards are listed for the game. Don't hesitate to try a game below your children's grade level. You might be surprised to discover that practice is needed in the highlighted skill. And you can certainly try a game above grade level. If it proves to be too difficult, change it or move on to a more suitable game.

Common Core State Standards

Professionals connected to the education of children are very aware of the Common Core State Standards, but if you're not a teacher or an education administrator, they may be new to you. Educators and other experts developed the Common Core Standards based on research and lessons learned from top-performing countries. (The *Common Core State Standards for Mathematics* (NGA Center and CCSSO 2010) can be downloaded for printing at http://www.corestandards.org/assets/CCSSI_Math%20Standards.pdf.) The standards describe the skills and knowledge children need to succeed in a rapidly changing world, including the ability to think creatively, solve real-world problems, make effective arguments, and engage in debates.

When it is appropriate, the number(s) of the exact standard(s) addressed by each game is indicated. If a game does not list one, that game was not designed to meet a specific standard at that grade level but developed to help children with concepts and skills that may need solidifying as well as with memory, visual discrimination, and critical thinking.

Many of the games include some of my observations and comments. After playing these games countless times with hundreds of children, I've discovered that there were certain patterns of thinking and behaviors that almost always occurred. I share them here as one teacher to another and as one parent to another so you can benefit from what I've learned playing these games and to provide a starting point for your own observations.

Questions promote reflection and help children make mathematical connections. Good questioning involves responding to a child in a manner that helps them think and makes you aware of what they are thinking. Because this can be a challenge at first, I have included some questions in each game that I have often used and that have proven to be effective.

Helpful hints for playing the games

- **It is very important that you use the correct mathematical language with children.** Speaking and understanding the language of math is a central part of learning important concepts in math. Use the correct terms from the very beginning. You can connect the words to concepts or ideas that children are already familiar with. Talk about *sums* (the answer to an addition problem) or *differences* (the answer to a subtraction problem), and so on. In other words, talk the talk while you play the games. To help you do so, chapters requiring familiarity with specific math terms have a glossary.

- **When playing games, children need to take responsibility for keeping each other accountable.** I've found that the best way to accomplish this is to have players exchange papers and check each other's work. If a player has calculated correctly, the other player puts his or her initials by the calculation. If there is a mistake, it is not initialed, but given back to the player to correct the mistake, or you may have the children work together to resolve the error. Parents playing with their children can check each other's work, too. What fun it is when a child finds a miscalculation in a parent's work!

- **Use counters.** Many games require counters. Anything will do—pennies, buttons, paper clips, pebbles, and such. I have found that the round transparent counters available at education supply stores work the best. They allow the players to see what's under the counters.

- If you are making game cards, make sure to print them on a medium-dark card stock or paper so that they cannot be read when facedown.

- **Make sure that players keep rotating turns.** Many other games allow the player who finds a pair to go again. That is not an effective strategy for keeping both players engaged. The games in this book don't allow for repeat turns.

- **Ask for student input.** Once a game has been played and mastered, ask your children how that game might be changed or made more challenging, and then give it a try! Or go on to the variation or the next game.

Game resources and materials

Many of the games feature game boards, recording sheets, or cards. These materials are available for downloading and printing as full-size blackline masters at NCTM's More4U online resource center. Simply go to www.nctm.org/more4u and enter the access code that is on the first page of this book.

Playing cards

After working with children for many years, I developed a set of ten-frame cards that I think are far more helpful for playing card games with children than a standard deck of playing cards.

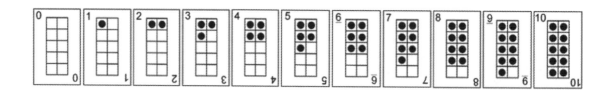

- These cards include 0 (zero) and regular decks do not. Zero is a very important number concept in our base-ten system and should not be left out of most games. Turning a queen, for example, into a 0 is not helpful when playing number games with children.

- This deck includes a 1 card. It is not always easy for children to visualize an ace as the number 1.

- The cards use a ten-frame, which shows a concrete representation of the amount each number represents; for example, a 7 has seven dots that are easily countable. It also anchors children to 10. The 7 shows seven dots and three blank spaces, so children can easily see and count how many more are needed to make 10.

- The cards are helpful in identifying odd and even numbers. If every dot has a partner, it is an even number. If one dot does not have a partner, it is an odd number.

The ten-frame deck of cards is like any other deck of cards in that there are four of each number in every deck.

Any standard deck of playing cards will be adequate, but I strongly recommend that you print and use the ten-frame cards on the National Council of Teachers of Mathematics More4U web page (www.nctm.org/more4u).

1. Print the cards on a medium-dark card stock (I use salmon). Don't use white or any other really light colors. You don't want players to be able to see the numbers when the cards are facedown.

2. Laminate them if possible. Many education supply stores have laminating machines. This really helps with longevity.

3. Cut them apart and begin to play.

If you use a standard deck of playing cards, remove the face cards. None of the games in the book need face cards.

Shuffling is very hard for children to do. It is all right to lay the cards facedown on a hard surface and mix them up. Making a neat pile might be a challenge for some children or it might take a good deal of time. Pushing the cards into a messy pile is completely acceptable. Players can choose a card from anywhere in the pile.

Dice

I also recommend that children use a big, heavy-duty paper plate for rolling dice. The paper plate softens the sound (most important in a classroom) and acts as a boundary for the dice. There are those eager-to-experiment children who want to roll the dice as far and as high as they can. The rule is that if a player rolls the die and it goes outside the plate, that player loses a turn.

The Games

Simple Addition

Introduction

    Addition Glossary 20

Adding to 10

    Pyramid 21

    Addition Ladder 23

    What Does It Take to Get to 10? 25

Adding to 20

    What Does It Take to Get to 12? 26

    Addition War 27

    Salute Addition 28

    Balancing Both Sides 30

    Four-in-a-Row—Sums to 18 32

    Get Close to 20 34

    The Constant Addend 36

    21 37

Adding to 30 and Higher

    Four-in-a-Row—Sums to 42 33

    Get Close to 25 35

    It Takes 5 to Make 25 38

    31 39

Introduction

It is important that children understand the relationship between addition and subtraction, and in the classroom, teaching these operations simultaneously recognizes the inverse relationship between the two operations. *I completely agree with this approach.* However, for the purpose of this book, they are treated in two separate chapters.

To quote the Common Core Standards for Mathematical Content, "By the end of Grade 2, (children should) know from memory all sums of two one-digit numbers" (2010, p. 19). I like to include addition facts for 10 as well: 10 + 0, 9 + 1, 8 + 2, 7 + 3, 6 + 4, 5 + 5, 4 + 6, 3 + 7, 2 + 8, 1 + 9, 0 + 10, and so on.

In my work with third, fourth, and fifth graders, it is not uncommon to encounter students who still struggle to master basic addition facts. They resort to counting on their fingers because they do not have these facts in instant recall. This is appropriate for younger children but not effective in the upper grades, and success in math is hampered. Fluency with small numbers is critical to proficiency with large numbers.

Children usually need to practice any addition fact *at least* two hundred times before it goes into long-term memory and can be instantly recalled. The following addition games provide enough active repetition so that the facts are more easily (and happily) learned. Try all of them—you and the children are bound to find favorites to play again and again. The games are sequenced from easiest to more challenging.

Addition Glossary

When playing math games, it is important that the children become familiar with the correct math terminology for certain facts and concepts. In this section there are four words that should be introduced and consistently used; their definitions are below.

Addend is any number added to another to get a sum or total.

Sum is the total (whole amount) realized as a result of adding numbers (addends).

Equal is having the same amount or identical value.

Equation, sometimes called a number sentence, is a mathematical statement containing an equals sign which shows that two expressions are equal.

addend		addend	equals sign	sum
3	+	7	=	10

addend		addend	equals sign	addend		addend
4	+	3	=	5	+	2

Pyramid

This is a solitaire game. The object is to have the lowest feasible score by removing as many cards from the pyramid as possible.

One-digit addition

Grade 3: CCSS.3.NBT.A.2
Grade 4
Grade 5

One player

Materials

- ten-frame cards, or standard deck with face cards removed

How to play

The cards are shuffled. Starting at the top of the pyramid, twenty-one cards are arranged faceup in a six-row pyramid with each row overlapping the preceding row. A sample pyramid is below.

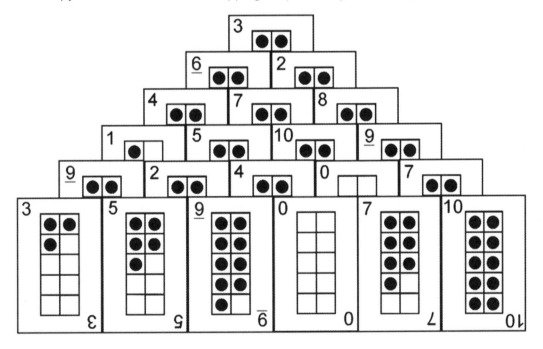

The remaining cards are placed facedown in a stack.

When children are first learning this game, they will need adult supervision when creating the pyramid, but the children should always be the ones actually building it. As with most tasks, the more often they do it themselves, the better they will be at making it.

Two conditions must be met before a card can be removed:

1. A card must be fully exposed with both bottom corners visible to be playable. When the game begins, only the six cards in the bottom row meet this requirement.

2. Cards can only be removed that equal 10 when added together.

Example

In the sample pyramid above, only the following cards can be removed:

the 7 and the 3 (7 + 3 = 10)

the 10 and the 0 (10 + 0 = 10)

After taking the 7, 3, 10, and 0 off the pyramid, there are only four cards that are fully exposed with both bottom corners visible, and none of them combine to equal 10. At this point, no other cards can be removed.

When there are no longer any exposed cards that when added together equal 10, the cards in the facedown stack are used. One card at a time is turned over. It can be used to pair with any fully exposed card in the pyramid to equal 10. If the new card does not combine to equal 10, it is placed in a discard pile, and another card is taken from the facedown stack and the process is repeated.

The game ends when all the cards in the facedown stack have been turned over. A player's score is the number of cards remaining in the pyramid—the fewer cards remaining in the pyramid, the better.

With each game, players try to have fewer cards remaining in the pyramid than in previous games. It is possible to remove all the cards in the pyramid, but it doesn't happen very often.

When children know the combinations of numbers that equal 10, the 10s are taken out of the deck, and a new pyramid is built with the object of finding combinations that equal 9.

Once the children learn the combinations equal to 9, the 9s are taken out of the deck and a pyramid to practice the combinations for 8 can be built; however, because the deck is reduced in size, make a smaller pyramid of five rows rather than six.

You can also build the pyramid using six rows to look for combinations that equal 11, 12, or 13.

> At some point, a child might begin to notice that three cards equal 10, such as 6 + 2 + 2. Great! They've noticed an important mathematical concept! Never tell them that this might be a possibility; allow them to discover it for themselves, and then let them share their discovery with the rest of the players!

Questions

Every time a new card is exposed, ask these questions:

- What do you need to go with that ____?

- Looking at the uncovered cards in the pyramid, what numbers do you hope will be turned over from the stack?

Addition Ladder

The goal of this game is to create addition equations that allow a player to put an equation on all the rungs of the "ladder."

One-digit addition

Grade 3: CCSS.3.NBT.A.2
Grade 4
Grade 5

Two players

Materials

- ten-frame cards, or standard deck with face cards removed

- paper

- pencils

- "Addition Ladder" recording sheet for each player

	= 9
	= 8
	= 7
	= 6
	= 5
	= 4
	= 3
	= 2
	= 1

How to play

The cards are shuffled and placed facedown in a stack.

Player 1 takes five cards and puts them faceup in a line. He uses two of the cards to make an equation that has a sum of 1 to 9 and writes that equation on his ladder on the appropriate rung. Player 1 then discards the two used cards.

Example

Player 1 has cards 7, 9, 1, 4, and 3. He makes the equation 4 + 3 = 7 and writes it on the 7 rung of his ladder.

	= 9
	= 8
4 + 3	= 7
	= 6
	= 5
	= 4
	= 3
	= 2
	= 1

Player 1 puts the two used cards, 4 and 3, in a discard pile.

Player 2 takes five cards from the stack and proceeds in the same manner.

Before each subsequent turn, players draw two more cards from the facedown stack so that they always have five cards to work with.

Players can put only one equation on each line. If a player cannot use her cards to place an equation on an empty line, she picks two cards from her faceup cards to put in the discard pile and loses her turn.

If players run out of cards in the facedown stack, they reshuffle the discard pile, stack it face-down, and continue to play.

Players alternate turns until one player wins by filling in all nine rungs on his ladder.

Questions

- What did you discover while playing this game?

- Where there any sums that were more difficult to make? Why?

- What equations could you use that would equal ____?

- What strategy might you try for the next game?

What Does It Take to Get to 10?

The goal of this game is to be the first player to cover three numbers in a vertical, horizontal, or diagonal row.

One-digit addition with a missing addend

Grade 3: CCSS.3.NBT.A.2

Grade 4

Grade 5

Two players

Materials

- one die

- counters

- "What Does It Take to Get to 10?" game board for each player

4	6	9	7
8	7	5	4
6	4	9	5
7	5	6	8

How to play

Player 1 rolls the die, and figures out what number is needed to get to 10, that is, the difference between the number rolled and 10. He places a counter on that game-board number and verbalizes the equation.

Example

Player 1 rolls a 4. A 6 is needed to get to 10. Player 1 covers one of the 6s on the game board and says, "Four plus six equals ten."

Player 2 rolls the die and proceeds in the same manner.

Players alternate turns until one player wins by placing three counters in a vertical, horizontal, or diagonal row.

Questions

- How did you figure out how many more you needed to get to 10?

- Can you convince me that if you have _____ , you need _____ to get to 10?

Variation: Use the "What Does It Take to Get to 12?" game board to play the game for addition to 12.

8	7	10	7
6	8	9	11
10	9	10	8
7	11	6	9

Addition War

The object of the game is to draw two addends cards whose sum is greater than the sum of the two addends of the other player.

One-digit addition
Variation: One-digit addition with three addends

Grade 3: CCSS.3.NBT.A.2
Grade 4
Grade 5

Two players

Materials

- ten-frame cards, or standard deck with face cards removed

How to play

The cards are shuffled and placed facedown in a stack.

Player 1 turns over two cards and adds the numbers. He verbalizes the equation to the other player, for example, "Four plus three equals seven." (Make sure the players give the entire equation, not just the sum.) Player 2 turns over two cards and proceeds in the same manner.

The player whose cards add up to the greater sum gets all four of the cards. In the event each player has the same sum, players turn over one more card and add that to their total. The greater sum wins all six cards.

Play continues until all the cards in the facedown stack have been used. Players count their cards, and the player with more accumulated cards is the winner.

Questions

- Prove to me that you have the greater sum.
- What number would you need to have a sum greater than the other player?
- How is it that you have the same sums, but you have different addends?

Variation: "Three Card Addition War" is played in the same way, but each player turns over three cards and finds the sum. In the event of a tie, each player takes a fourth card and adds that number to her total.

Salute Addition

The goal of the game is to discover the unknown addend.

One-digit addition with a missing addend

Grade 3: CCSS.3.NBT.A.2
Grade 4
Grade 5

Two players

Materials

- ten-frame cards, or standard deck with face cards removed

How to play

The cards are shuffled and placed facedown in a stack.

Player 1 turns over the top card and verbalizes the number, then places it faceup so that Player 2 can see it.

Player 2 draws a card (the "salute" card) and, without looking at it, holds the card to her forehead so that Player 1 can see it, but she can't.

Player 1 adds the two cards mentally and verbalizes the addition equation without giving the salute number on Player 2's forehead; for example, "Four plus the number on your forehead equals ten."

Player 2 must figure out what the card on her forehead must be and says that number out loud; in this case, it is 6.

> Player 2 might be thinking, "I know the first number is four, but I don't know what the number on my forehead is. If the two numbers equal ten, then I must have a six on my forehead because four plus six equals ten."

If Player 2 answers correctly, she takes both cards. If Player 2 is not correct, she must continue until she figures out the missing addend; however, she will not get to keep the two cards. They are put in a discard pile.

Players reverse roles, and play continues until all the facedown cards have been used. The player with more accumulated cards wins the game.

Questions

- How did you figure out what the number on your head was?

- What facts do you need to practice?

This is one of my very favorite games! When we help children learn these very important facts to 10, we almost always ask, "What does two plus three equal?" Good to know, but it is also very helpful to teach addition using the missing addend approach, "What number when added to two equals five?"

Once children become fairly good at this game, I find it is important to transfer the equations to paper or board. I explain the "n" means mystery number, and then I ask the students a series of questions, writing everything on the board so they can see it:

- $5 + n = 9$ What's the mystery number?
- $n + 5 = 9$ What's the mystery number?
- $4 + n = 9$ What's the mystery number?
- $n + 4 = 9$ What's the mystery number?
- $5 + 4 = n$ What's the mystery number?

When they get really good at this, I begin to make the equations more difficult. Here are a few examples:

- $3 + 4 = 6 + n$
- $1 + 6 = 4 + n$
- $9 + 0 = 5 + n$
- $2 + n = 1 + 4$

This game helps children look at and understand what the equal sign means. Too often children only see $4 + 5 = n$ and think that the equal sign means "now find the answer." They need to understand that it means that the equation must be balanced, or have the same value on each side.

Balancing Both Sides

The object of the game is to balance both sides of the equation by arranging the cards into two addition problems with equal sums.

One-digit addition

Grade 3: CCSS.3.NBT.A.2
Grade 4
Grade 5

Two players

Materials

- ten-frame cards, or standard deck with face cards removed
- "Balancing Both Sides" game board for each player

_____ + _____ = _____ + _____

How to play

A player earns one point for balancing both sides of the equation.

Player 1 shuffles the cards and deals eight cards to each player. (Players take turns being the dealer.) The remaining cards are stacked facedown.

Player 1 chooses four cards from her hand of eight to place on the game board to create an equal equation. (Players must use at least four cards.) Before taking his turn, Player 2 must check and make sure that Player 1 has balanced both sides of the equation. If so, Player 1 gets one point; she puts her eight cards on the bottom of the deck.

Example

Player 1 has a 9, 7, 4, 5, 4, 3, 1, and 8. She could place 7 + 1 on one side of the equation and 3 + 5 on the other. Player 2 checks the equation. Each side equals 8 so both sides of the equation have the same value and the game board is balanced. Player 1 earns one point.

Player 2 chooses four cards from his hand of eight cards to place on his board, and proceeds in the same manner.

Sometimes the eight cards cannot be combined for a balanced equation. That player loses a turn. At other times there is more than one right combination using the eight cards. In the example above, Player 1 could have also made 5 + 3 = 4 + 4 or 4 + 4 = 7 + 1.

Player 2 shuffles the cards and deals eight new cards to each player. Play continues in the same way.

Players alternate turns, always checking each other's equation to make sure it is balanced. The game ends when one player reaches ten points.

Questions

- What did you notice while playing this game?

- What does the left side of the number sentence equal? The right side? Is the equation balanced? Do both sides of the equation have the same value?

- Is there another way this could be set up using different numbers and still be balanced?

Four-in-a-Row—Sums to 18

This game generates a lot of practice in mental addition. The goal of the game is to have four counters in a vertical, horizontal, or diagonal row.

One-digit addition
Variation: Two-digit addition

Grade 3: CCSS.3.NBT.A.2
Grade 4
Grade 5

Two players

Materials

- two paper clips
- different counters for each player
- "Four-in-a-Row—Sums to 18" game board

17	2	14	3	8
7	5	0	13	18
1	10	15	6	9
12	8	6	4	7
4	5	3	11	16

0   1   2   3   4   5   6   7   8   9

How to play

Player 1 places two paper clips under any one or two of the addends in the line below the game grid. (The two paper clips can be placed under the same addend.)

Player 1 adds the two marked addends, places a counter on the corresponding sum on the game board, and verbalizes the equation.

From this point on, only one paper clip can be moved.

Player 2 moves one paper clip to a new addend. She adds these two addends, places a counter on the corresponding sum on the game board, and verbalizes the equation.

Example

Player 1 places one paper clip under the 2 and the other under the 6 in the addend line; he adds 2 + 6, places a counter on one of the 8s on his game board, and verbalizes the equation. Player

2 leaves one paper clip on the 2 and moves the other paper clip to the 9; she adds 2 + 9, puts a counter on the 11 on her game board, and verbalizes the equation.

If a sum already has a counter on it, another counter may not be put on top.

Players alternate turns until one player has four counters in a vertical, horizontal, or diagonal row.

To introduce this game in the classroom, I play it with the whole class. I use a document camera to project the game board, including the addend line.

I divide the class in half and assign different colors to each side; for instance, the left side of the room (red) plays against the right side of the room (blue). I have found that round transparent counters work best. (I'm often asked how I decide which team goes first. There are many possibilities. I always respond, "This is no longer my game. It's yours. You decide. Do what works best for your children.")

One team begins the game by telling me where to put the two paper clips.

I usually take the first suggestion I hear, but not always. The child must give me a full equation, for example, "Put the first paper clip under the four and the second under the six. Four plus six equals ten." So I put that team's counter on the 10.

The other team has its turn, but it can move only one paper clip. Again, I usually take the first suggestion I hear.

At some point, the students on each team begin to disagree about which paper clip should be moved. I give them a short amount of time (a minute at most) to get organized, talk about possible strategies, and decide how they are going to proceed.

Once the game is learned as a class, I pair the children to play against each other.

Questions

- After looking at the counters already on the board, which sums would be helpful because they would put a counter next to another counter you already have on the board? What addends could you use to get that sum?

- What sums would help you block the other player from getting four in a row?

Variation: "Four-in-a-Row—Sums to 42" is played using the game board below.

18	19	20	21	22
23	24	25	26	27
28	29	30	31	32
33	34	35	36	37
38	39	40	41	42

9   10   11   12   13   14   15   16   17   18   19   20   21

Get Close to 20

The object of the game is to make an addition problem with three addends whose sum is as close to 20 as possible. The sum can be more or less than 20.

Addition with three addends
Variation: Addition with four addends

Grade 3: CCSS.3.NBT.A.2
Grade 4
Grade 5

Two players

Materials

- ten-frame cards, or standard deck with face cards removed
- "Get Close to 20" recording sheet for each player

Round	Equation	Points for round
1	+ + =	
2	+ + =	
3	+ + =	
4	+ + =	
5	+ + =	
	Total points for game	

How to play

The cards are shuffled and placed facedown in a stack.

Player 1 takes five cards and uses the numbers on any *three* of the cards to equal a sum that is as close to 20 as possible. Each card can be used only once. Player 1 writes the equation on the recording sheet and puts the five cards in a discard pile.

The points for each round are the *difference* between the sum and 20. For example, a sum of 24 scores 4 points; a sum of 16 also scores 4 points.

Player 2 draws five cards and proceeds in the same manner.

When there are no more cards in the facedown stack, the discard pile is shuffled, stacked face-down, and play continues.

After five rounds, players find the sum of all their points, and the player with the least sum wins.

Questions

- You have five cards, but you can only use three of them. Which three cards will get you as close to 20 as you can get?

- Will another combination of three cards get you any closer? Try out some combinations.

- Which two cards don't you need? Why is that?

- Did you find any strategy that helped you get as close to 20 as possible? Which numbers did you find to be helpful? Which numbers were not helpful?

Variation: Change the game to "Get Close to 25." Players take six cards from the facedown stack for each round and can use any four cards to get a sum as close to 25 as possible.

The Constant Addend

The goal of the game is to have the greater sum.

One-digit addition

Grade 3: CCSS.3.NBT.A.2
Grade 4
Grade 5

Two players

Materials

- ten-frame cards, or standard deck with face cards removed

How to play

Players are seated side by side, not face to face.

The teacher, parent, or players decide which particular addition fact to practice, such as +3, +4, +9, and so on. Once the constant addend is determined, a card with that number is taken from the deck and placed between the two players.

Player 1 shuffles the cards and divides them evenly facedown between himself and Player 2. (Players take turns being the dealer.)

Player 1 turns over his top card, adds it to the constant addend, and verbalizes the sum. Player 2 turns over her top card and proceeds in the same manner. The player with the greater sum takes both cards.

Example

It is decided that players need to practice +7. They take one 7 out of the deck and place it faceup between each other. This 7 is the constant addend in each round. Player 1 turns over a 5, adds it to the 7 in the middle, and says, "Five plus seven equals twelve." Player 2 turns over an 8, adds it to the 7, and says, "Eight plus seven equals fifteen." Player 2 collects both cards.

> Players must verbalize the equation. If they don't, they won't actually have to do any addition. They will simply note who turned over the bigger number, and take both cards based on that.

In the event of a tie (both players have the same sum), players turn over one more card and add that number to their previous sum. The player with the greater sum collects all four cards.

The constant addend card (a 7 in the above example) remains in the middle until all the facedown cards have been used; then players count their cards. The player with more cards is the winner.

Questions

- How did you figure out _____ + _____?

- What do you already know? What do you need to practice?

21

This game is intended to be a mental math addition game—paper and pencil are not involved. Players are expected to do the addition in their heads as they try to reach 21 without going over that sum.

Mental addition

Grade 3: CCSS.3.NBT.A.2

Grade 4

Grade 5

Two players

Materials

- ten-frame cards, or standard deck with face cards removed

How to play

The cards are shuffled. Each player receives one card facedown and then one card faceup. (Players take turns being the dealer.)

Keeping their facedown card from the view of the other player, players peek at it and mentally find the sum of their two cards.

A player may ask for more cards, but must be careful not to exceed the total of 21.

The player whose hand is closest to 21, without going over, is the winner and gets one point.

If the players have the same sum, no one gets a point. Play continues until one player gets ten points.

> If children have never played this game, it is advisable to play several rounds with all cards faceup so they can see what they are expected to do.

Questions

Guide the children through the game with the following questions:

- What is the sum of your numbers now?
- How many do you need to reach 21?
- What number would be best to get?
- Which numbers would get you closer to 21 but not there exactly?
- Which cards would put you over 21?

It Takes 5 to Make 25

This game is intended to be a mental math addition game—paper and pencil are not involved. Players are expected to do the addition in their heads as they add and discard cards to obtain a hand of five cards that equals 25 exactly.

Mental addition

Grade 3: CCSS.3.NBT.A.2
Grade 4
Grade 5

Two players

Materials

* ten-frame cards, or standard deck with face cards removed

How to play

The cards are shuffled and five cards are dealt to each player. (Players take turns being the dealer.) The remaining cards are stacked facedown; the top card is turned faceup and placed to the side of the stack to begin a discard pile.

Player 1 adds up the numbers of the cards in her hand, and then takes one card from either the facedown stack or the discard pile. She discards one card.

Player 2 adds up the numbers of the cards in his hand, draws one card, and proceeds in the same manner.

Players alternate turns until one player has a hand whose numbers add up to exactly 25. The player must declare, "Twenty-five." Both players check that the five cards really do have a sum of 25. If they do, that player wins the game.

Questions

* What did you discover while playing this game?
* At this very moment in the game, what will get you exactly to 25?
* Anything else? Which two cards might get you there?
* What will get you close to 25 but not quite there?
* Are there any numbers you don't need because they will take you over 25?
* What do you notice about the five numbers that finally added up to 25?

31

This is intended to be a mental math addition game. In other words, paper and pencil are not involved. Players must do the addition in their heads as they try to reach exactly 31.

Mental addition

Grade 3: CCSS.3.NBT.A.2
Grade 4
Grade 5

Two players

Materials

- different counters for each player
- "31" game board

1	2	3	4	5	6
1	2	3	4	5	6
1	2	3	4	5	6
1	2	3	4	5	6

How to play

Player 1 puts a counter on any number. Player 2 also puts a counter on any number, adding this number to Player 1's number. Player 1 then puts a counter on a third number, adding it to the previous sum.

Players alternate turns, adding their number to the previous sum of all the marked numbers.

The player who puts a counter on a number that results in the sum of exactly 31 is the winner. If a player places a counter on a number that makes a sum over 31, the other player wins.

Questions

Here are a few questions to ask players as the sums get closer to 31:

- Did you discover any strategies that might help you win the next time?
- What number will get you to exactly 31?
- Which numbers will get you closer to 31 but not quite there?
- Which numbers will you not be able to use because they will take you over 31?

The Games

Place Value

Introduction

Place Value Glossary 42

Creating and Comparing Two-Digit Numbers

Two-Digit War 43

Caught in the Middle 46

Close to 50 48

Expanded Form 50

Creating and Comparing Three-Digit Numbers

Three-Digit War 45

Three-Digit Caught in the Middle 47

Close to 500 49

Three-Digit Expanded Form 51

Creating and Comparing Four-Digit Numbers

Four-Digit War 45

Four-Digit Caught in the Middle 47

Close to 5,000 49

Four-Digit Expanded Form 51

Creating and Comparing Five-Digit Numbers

Whose Is Greater? 52

To Trade or Not to Trade? 54

Creating And Comparing Seven-Digit Numbers

The Million Game 56

Introduction

Many children, and even some adults, have difficulty comprehending the abstract concept of place value. To understand place value is to understand the structure and sequence of our base-ten number system. As children count, interpret the values of written and spoken numbers, decide which number is larger or smaller, and explore relationships among numbers, they are developing a mental picture of our number system.

When children count, they basically learn numbers as a never-ending sequence that goes on and on. With simple counting, children might not catch on to the inherent structure of our base-ten number system. They can count thirteen objects, but they do not see that thirteen is one group of ten and three ones.

Playing the following math games will enable children to develop a deeper understanding of place value.

Place Value Glossary

When playing any math games, it is important that the children become familiar with the correct math terminology for certain facts and concepts. In this section there is one word that is used in many of the games. It should be consistently used; its definition is below.

Digit is a symbol (numeral) used to indicate a numeric value. For example—

- 8 is a one-digit number;
- 18 is a two-digit number; and
- 180 is a three-digit number.

Two-Digit War

The goal of each round of this game is to be the player with the greater two-digit number.

Creating and comparing two-digit numbers
Variation 1: Creating and comparing two-digit numbers
Variation 2: Creating and comparing three-digit numbers
Variation 3: Creating and comparing four-digit numbers

Grade 3
Grade 4: CCSS.4.NBT.A.2
Grade 5

Two players

Materials

- ten-frame cards with 10s removed, or standard deck with 10s and face cards removed

- "Two-Digit War" game board for each player

Tens	Ones

How to play

The cards are shuffled and placed facedown in a stack.

Player 1 turns over one card and decides whether to put it in the tens or ones column on his board. The card must be placed before the other player can take a turn, and once down, it cannot be moved.

Player 2 turns over one card and decides whether to put it in the tens or ones column on her board.

Player 1 turns over a second card and puts it in the empty column. Player 2 turns over a second card and does the same.

Players read their numbers out loud to each other, using the number of the card in each column to express tens and ones.

Example

Player 1 says, "I have 8 tens and 7 ones. I have eighty-seven." Player 2 says, "I have 7 tens and 2 ones. I have seventy-two."

The player with the greater two-digit number takes all four cards. If players have exactly the same number, they each take their two cards back.

Have the children make a record of each turn by recording both numbers using the greater than, less than, or equal to symbols (see the sample below).

Round	Player 1	>=<	Player 2
Sample	87	>	72
Sample	45	<	47
Sample	53	=	53

Play continues until all the cards in the stack have been used. Players count their accumulated cards, and the player with more cards wins.

Questions

- Have you found a strategy that helps you create a greater two-digit number?
- In order to win this round, what number will your second card need to be?
- Are there any numbers that will be helpful?
- Are there any numbers that will not be helpful?
- You say you're hoping for a _____. How likely is it that you will draw a _____?

Variation 1: The game is played in the same way, but the player with the smaller two-digit number wins.

Variation 2: Modify the game to play "Three-Digit War." Each player takes three cards and tries to make the greater three-digit number using the game board below. Players read their numbers out loud to each other, using the number of the card in each column to express hundreds, tens, and ones.

Hundreds	Tens	Ones

Variation 3: To play "Four-Digit War" each player takes four cards and tries to make the greater four-digit number using the game board below. The rules of the game remain the same.

Thousands	Hundreds	Tens	Ones

Caught in the Middle

The goal of this game is to have the third two-digit number fall between a player's smallest two-digit number and greatest two-digit number.

Creating and comparing two-digit numbers
Variation 1: Creating and comparing three-digit numbers
Variation 2: Creating and comparing four-digit numbers

Grade 3
Grade 4
Grade 5

Two players

Materials

- ten-frame cards with 10s removed, or standard deck with 10s and face cards removed

- paper

- pencil

How to play

The cards are shuffled and stacked facedown.

Player 1 takes four cards to make two two-digit numbers. She uses two of the cards to make the smallest possible two-digit number, and then uses the remaining two cards to make the greatest two-digit number. Player 2 takes four cards and proceeds in the same manner.

Example

Player 1 draws a 6, 2, 7, and 1. She uses two of her numbers to make the smallest two-digit number she can, a 12. She uses the other two cards to make the greatest possible two-digit number, a 76. The range of Player 1's two numbers is 12 to 76. Player 2 draws a 5, 3, 1, and 4. He uses two of his numbers to make the smallest two-digit number he can, 13, and uses the other two cards to make the greatest two-digit number, 54. The range of Player 2's two numbers is 13 to 54.

After both players make their two-digit numbers, two more cards are turned over. The first card turned over is the tens number. The second card is the ones number.

Players only score a point if this new number falls between the two they have made.

Example

Using the example above, Player 1's range of numbers is 12 to 76, and Player 2's is 13 to 54. The last two cards turned over are a 6 for tens and a 2 for ones. The point number is therefore 62. Player 1 scores a point because 62 is between 12 and 76. Player 2 does not score a point because 62 does not fall between 13 and 54.

All the cards are put in a discard pile. Players draw four more cards and proceed as above. When all the cards in the facedown stack have been used, the discard pile is shuffled and play continues.

Players alternate turns. The first player to reach twenty points is the winner.

Variation 1: "Three-Digit Caught in the Middle" is played in the same manner, but players draw six cards and create two three-digit numbers with as wide a range as possible.

Variation 2: "Four-Digit Caught in the Middle" is played in the same manner, but players draw eight cards and create two four-digit numbers with as wide a range as possible.

Place Value

Close to 50

The goal of this game is to create a two-digit number that is as close to 50 as possible. This is not an "exact" game, so numbers can be more or less than 50.

Creating and comparing two-digit numbers
Variation 1: Creating and comparing three-digit numbers
Variation 2: Creating and comparing four-digit numbers

Grade 3
Grade 4
Grade 5

Two players

Materials

- ten-frame cards with 10s removed, or standard deck with 10s and face cards removed

- paper

- pencils

How to play

The cards are shuffled and placed facedown in a stack.

Player 1 takes two cards, and basing her decision on which of the two numbers will be closest to 50, Player 1 chooses which card will be the tens and which card will be the ones.

Example

Player 1 draws a 4 and an 8. She knows she can make 48 or 84, and decides to make 48 because that is closer to 50 than 84.

Player 2 takes two cards from the stack and proceeds in the same manner.

Players' scores for the round are the difference between their two-digit number and 50. For example, a player with the number 46 would get a score of 4 as would a player with 54.

Players alternate turns until they have played six rounds. Players add their scores. The player with the lesser sum wins the game.

Questions

- Why did you choose _____ over _____?
- Convince me that _____ is closer to 50 than _____.
- What's the difference between _____ and 50?
- How did you figure out what the difference is between your number and 50?
- Which numbers might be closer to 50 than your number?

Children may need a hundred board and paper and pencil to figure out what the difference is between their number and 50. As a parent or teacher, don't be too ready to give them ways to figure this out. Ask them how they figure out what the difference is between _____ and 50?

If the number is less than 50, an adult's instinct about how the task should be done might be to subtract that number from 50 to find the difference. For example, 50 – 32 = 18; or if the number is greater than 50, to subtract 50 from that number; for instance, 84 – 50 = 34. But many children (and adults) might find it easier to count up from 32 to 50 or count up from 50 to 84. That's all right, too.

Variation 1: "Close to 500" is played in the same manner, but players take three cards from the facedown stack to create a number as close to 500 as possible.

Example

Player 1 draws 9, 3, and 4. The digits can be arranged to make 934, 943, 493, 439, 394, or 349. Player 1 chooses 493 because it is closest to 500.

Variation 2: "Close to 5,000" is played in the same manner, but players take four cards from the facedown stack to create a four-digit number as close to 5,000 as possible.

Expanded Form

The goal of this game is to accurately describe two-digit numbers

Expanded form for two-digit numbers
Variation 1: Expanded form for three-digit numbers
Variation 2: Expanded form for four-digit numbers

Grade 3
Grade 4: CCSS.4.NBT.A.2
Grade 5

Two players

Materials

- ten-frame cards with 10s removed, or standard deck with 10s and face cards removed

- pencils

- "Expanded Form" recording sheet for each player

Number	Tens	Ones	Number Words	Expanded Form

How to play

The cards are shuffled and stacked facedown.

Player 1 takes two cards and decides which two-digit number to make. He records this number on his sheet, breaks out tens and ones, writes the number in words, and records the number in its expanded form. Player 2 checks the entry for accuracy. Each correct answer is worth one point; if all the answers are correct, the entry earns a total of five points.

Example

Player 1 draws 7 and 4. He knows he can make 74 or 47, and decides to make 74. He records the number in the following way:

Player 2 makes sure each answer is correct. Player 1 earns one point for each correct answer; he gains five points for this entry.

Number	Tens	Ones	Number Words	Expanded Form
74	7	4	seventy-four	70 + 4

After scoring is completed, players must correct any errors.

Player 2 takes two cards and proceeds in the same manner.

The first player to reach fifty points is the winner.

Questions

- What was difficult about this game? What was easy?

- How is the number _____ different than _____? Could you illustrate or demonstrate how they are different?

Variation 1: "Three-Digit Expanded Form" is similar but players take three cards to create and record a three-digit number.

Number	Hundreds	Tens	Ones	Number Words	Expanded Form

Variation 2: "Four-Digit Expanded Form" The game is played in the same manner but players take four cards to make and record a four-digit number.

Whose Is Greater?

The goal of this game is to create the greater five-digit number.

Creating and comparing five-digit numbers

Grade 3
Grade 4: CCSS.4.NBT.A.2
Grade 5

Two players

Materials

- ten-frame cards with 10s removed,
  or standard deck with 10s and face cards removed
- "Whose Is Greater?" recording sheet for each player

Round	10,000s	1,000s	100s	10s	1s	Number
1						
2						
3						
4						
5						
6						

How to play

The cards are shuffled and placed facedown in a stack.

Player 1 draws a card. Both players write that number in one of the place-value positions for round 1. Each player must write the number down immediately. Once a number is written down, it cannot be moved or changed.

Player 2 draws a second card, and both players write that number in one of the remaining place-value positions in round 1.

Players continue to alternate turns drawing a card until all five place-value positions in the round 1 row are filled.

The Games

Example

Round	10,000s	1,000s	100s	10s	1s	Number
1	6 (60,000)	4 (4,000)	3 (300)	7 (70)	5	64,375

Players read their numbers to each other. The player with the greater number scores a point. At the end of six rounds, the player with more points wins the game.

Questions

- What did you discover while playing this game?

- Will that change how you play the game next time?

- Did you find any strategies that were helpful?

Variation: The game is played in the same way, but the player having the lesser five-digit number scores a point.

Place Value

To Trade or Not to Trade?

The goal of this game is to make the greater five-digit number. The game board uses word numbers for the columns so the children become familiar with them and their meanings.

Creating and comparing five-digit numbers

Grade 3
Grade 4: CCSS.4.NBT.A.2
Grade 5

Two players

Materials

- ten-frame cards with 10s removed, or standard deck with 10s and face cards removed

- "To Trade or Not to Trade?" game board for each player

Ten Thousands	Thousands	Hundreds	Tens	Ones

- "To Trade or Not to Trade?" recording sheet

Round	Player 1	< = >	Player 2
1			
2			
3			
4			
5			
6			

How to play

Players sit side by side so they can easily compare their numbers. The cards are shuffled and placed facedown in a stack.

Player 1 takes five cards and does not look at them. He places them facedown on his game board, one card per column. Player 1 turns over the card in the ones column and decides whether to keep the card or trade it for the top card of the facedown stack. If he decides to exchange the card, he cannot change his mind. He puts the replaced ones card in a discard pile.

Player 2 draws five cards and proceeds in the same manner.

Player 1 turns over the card in the tens column and decides whether to keep the card or trade it for the top card of the facedown pile.

Player 2 turns over the card in the tens column and proceeds in the same manner.

Continuing to alternate turns, the players determine the hundreds, thousands, and finally, the ten thousands place. Players write their five-digit numbers on the recording sheet, read their numbers to each other, and decide which symbol (greater than, less than, or equal to) should be used.

Round	Player 1	> = <	Player 2
1	47,621	<	53,953
2			
3			
4			
5			
6			

The player with the greater number scores one point. After six rounds, the player with more points wins the game.

Questions

- What strategy have you discovered that helps you build the greater number?

- What were you thinking when you decided to trade in that _____ in the ten-thousands place?

Variation: The game is played in the same way, but the goal is to build the least five-digit number.

The Million Game

This game gives students plenty of practice in verbalizing large numbers. Its goal is to make the greater seven-digit number and verbalize it correctly.

Creating and comparing seven-digit numbers

Grade 3
Grade 4: CCSS.4.NBT.A.2
Grade 5

Two players

Materials

- ten-frame cards with 10s removed, or standard deck with 10s and face cards removed

- "The Million Game" place-value cards for each player

Millions	Hundred Thousands	Ten Thousands	Thousands	Hundreds	Tens	Ones

- "The Million Game" recording sheet

Round	Player 1	Point	>=<	Player 2	Point
1					
2					
3					
4					
5					
6					

How to play

Players sit side by side so they can easily compare their numbers. Players organize their place-value cards to form a game board. The ten-frame cards are shuffled and stacked facedown.

Player 1 draws a card and places it faceup on any place-value position on his board. Player 2 draws a card and places it faceup in any place-value position on her board.

Players alternate turns until all the place-value positions are filled. Players read their numbers to each other.

> Reading the numbers aloud to each other may be the most important and the hardest part of this game. Students often struggle to do so, but as they continue to practice verbalizing the numbers, it becomes easier, and the children become more confident.

Players write their seven-digit numbers on the recording sheet and decide which symbol (greater than, less than, or equal to) should be used.

The player who has made the greater number and can verbalize it correctly gets one point. If a player makes the greater number, but does not verbalize it correctly, he does not get a point. At the end of six rounds, the player with more points wins the game.

Questions

- What did you discover while playing this round?
- Will you do anything differently the next round?
- What strategy was helpful? Why?
- How did you decide which number was greater and which was less?
- What is the difference between the two numbers?

Variation: The game is played in the same way, but the goal is to build and express the least seven-digit number.

The Games

Multidigit Addition

Introduction

Multidigit Addition Glossary 61

Adding Two Two-Digit Numbers

Double-Digit Addition 62

Concentration 100 64

Get Close to 105 66

Get as Close as You Can to 100 67

Adding Three Two-Digit Numbers

Triple Double-Digit Addition 63

Adding a Two-Digit Number to a Three-Digit Number

First One to 1,000 Wins 69

Adding Two Three-Digit Numbers

Three-Digit Addition 63

Get as Close as You Can to 1,000 68

Beat the Teacher 70

It All Adds Up 72

It All Adds Up to 500 73

Adding Two Four-Digit Numbers

Four-Digit Addition 63

Four-Digit It All Adds Up 73

Introduction

Because conceptual understanding of basic facts and place value are intrinsic to success in computing multidigit problems, the simple addition games and the place value games serve as preparation for the multidigit addition games in this chapter.

Many children in third, fourth, and fifth grades struggle to instantly recall basic addition facts like 4 + 5 = 9. This lack of recall slows them down considerably. Once they have figured out the basic fact, they can add multidigit numbers, but they don't seem to really understand the role of place value.

For example, in the number 47, the 4 is not a simple 4. It is 4 tens or 40. When presented with a problem such as

$$47$$
$$+\ 32$$

what children usually see is 7 plus 2, and then 4 plus 3, without any idea of the real value of the numbers.

Addition is the combining of values that are alike, so it's important to know what's being added. For example, which numbers are *hundreds*, *tens* and *ones*?

Having the basic facts in instant recall and understanding place value is crucial to children's future success in higher levels of mathematics.

One way to help children understand the concept of place value is to approach addition using a different technique. The method is called *partial-sums addition*. I like it because it helps keep place value front and center. It also helps children "see" and understand regrouping (carrying) more clearly.

Here are two examples using partial-sums addition. The first example starts in the traditional manner of adding the ones first:

$$47$$
$$+35$$
$$12\ (7+5)$$
$$+\ 70\ (40+30)$$
$$82$$

This example of partial-sums addition below adds the tens first. (Yes, it is possible to start with the tens first and get it right!)

$$47$$
$$+35$$
$$70\ (40+30)$$
$$+12\ (7+5)$$
$$82$$

Play the following multidigit addition games using the standard column method of adding multi-digit numbers, and see if the partial-sums strategy is at all helpful.

Multidigit Addition Glossary

When playing math games, it is important that the children become familiar with the correct math terminology for certain facts and concepts. In this section there are five words that should be consistently used; their definitions are below.

Addend is any number added to another to get a sum or total.

Sum is the total (whole amount) realized as a result of adding numbers (addends).

Digit is a symbol (numeral) used to indicate a numeric value. For example, 8 is a one-digit number, 18 is a two-digit number, and 180 is a three-digit number.

Equal is having the same amount or identical value.

Equation, sometimes called a number sentence, is a mathematical statement containing an equals sign that shows that two expressions are equal in value.

addend		addend	equals sign	sum		
31	+	16	=	47		

addend		addend	equals sign	addend		addend
40	+	30	=	50	+	20

Double-Digit Addition

The goal of this game is to create the greatest sum possible using four cards.

Two-digit addition
Variation 1: Two-digit addition
Variation 2: Adding 3 two-digit numbers
Variation 3: Three-digit addition
Variation 4: Four-digit addition

Grade 3: CCSS.3.NBT.A.2
Grade 4: CCSS.4.NBT.B.4
Grade 5

Two players

Materials

- ten-frame cards with 10s removed, or standard deck with 10s and face cards removed
- paper
- pencils

How to play

The cards are shuffled and placed facedown in a stack.

Player 1 takes four cards and makes two two-digit numbers that when added together will result in the greatest possible sum. Player 2 takes four cards and does the same. Both players write their numbers down and find their sums. Players exchange papers and check each other's addition. The player with the greater sum gets one point.

Example

Player 1 draws 4, 7, 1, and 8. She decides to make 74 and 81. Player 1 writes down the two numbers and adds them together:

$$\begin{array}{r} 74 \\ + 81 \\ \hline 155 \end{array}$$

Player 2 draws 9, 3, 2, and 5. He decides to make 52 and 93. Player 2 writes down the two numbers and adds them together:

$$\begin{array}{r} 52 \\ + 93 \\ \hline 145 \end{array}$$

Player 1 gets one point because she has the greater sum.

The first player to get ten points is the winner.

Questions

- Is there a way to use those same numbers and make two two-digit numbers that when added together will give you a greater sum? Move them around and see.

- How do you know your number is greater than the other player's number?

- Using the numbers 0 to 9, what is the largest possible sum you could make? The smallest?

Variation 1: The game is played in the same way, but the player with the smaller sum wins the point.

Variation 2: "Triple Double-Digit Addition" is played in the same way, but players take six cards to make three two-digit numbers with either greater or smaller sums.

Variation 3: "Three-Digit Addition" is played in the same way, but players take six cards to make two three-digit numbers with either greater or smaller sums.

Variation 4: "Four-Digit Addition" is played in the same way, but players take eight cards to make two four-digit numbers with either greater or smaller sums.

Concentration 100

The goal of this game is to find two numbers that when added together equal 100.

Two-digit addition

Grade 3: CCSS.3.NBT.A.2
Grade 4: CCSS.4.NBT.B.4
Grade 5

Two players

Materials

- "Concentration 100" addend cards

10	90	25	75	33	67
47	53	55	45	2	98
76	24	88	12	5	95
40	60	15	85	77	23
30	70	92	8	61	39

mor**4U**

- paper
- pencils

Pregame practice

The practice session with the cards *faceup* allows the children to see what they are expected to do mathematically.

The cards are shuffled and placed *faceup* in a grid of five rows with six cards in each row.

Player 1 finds two addend cards whose sum is 100 and sets them aside.

Player 2 finds two addend cards whose sum is 100 and sets them aside.

Players alternate turns until all the matches have been made.

Questions

- What do you need to go with that _____?
- What could you do to figure it out?
- Are there any combinations that you knew immediately equaled 100?

How to play

The cards are shuffled and placed *faceup* in a grid of five rows with six cards in each row.

Player 1 turns over one card, keeping it in place, and says the number out loud. She turns over a second card and says that number out loud. If the cards equal 100, Player 1 verbalizes the equation; for example, "Twenty-five plus seventy-five equals one hundred," and keeps both cards. If the cards do not equal 100, Player 1 tells Player 2 what they do equal, for instance, "Twenty-five plus thirty-three does not equal one hundred; they equal fifty-eight." She turns the cards back over, keeping them in the same place.

Player 2 turns over a card and proceeds in the same manner.

> When players find a match and keep both cards, they don't immediately get another turn as in some games. Players continue to alternate turns so both players stay engaged.

Players alternate turns until all the matches have been made. The winner is the player with more accumulated cards.

> When they first start to play this game, children may need to use paper and pencil to figure out which card they need. After playing the game a few times over several days, the paper and pencil may not be needed as often, if at all.

Questions

- After children have turned over the first addend, ask them which card they are looking for that when added to the first card will make a sum of 100.

- What can you do to figure out which card you need?

Get Close to 105

The object of the game is to get a final score that is closer to 105 than the other player's. Players must complete ten full rounds of play in order to win.

Two-digit addition

Grade 3: CCSS.3.NBT.A.2
Grade 4: CCSS.4.NBT.B.4
Grade 5

Two players

Materials

- three dice
- paper
- pencils

How to play

Player 1 rolls the three dice. He adds them together and puts the sum as his score for that round.

Player 2 rolls the dice and does the same.

Players alternate turns, adding the current sum of the three dice to their previous sum.

At the end of ten rounds, the player with the score closest to 105 wins the game.

Questions

- Your sum was considerably higher than 105. Why do you think that happened?
- Your sum was considerably less than 105. Why do you think that happened?
- How far is your sum from 105?
- How did you figure it out?
- How do you know that _____ is closer to 105?
- Is there a target score that will be too high for three dice and ten rounds?

Variation: Players can change the target number to any number equal to or less than 180, and play the game the same way.

Get as Close as You Can to 100

The object of the game is to create a two-digit addition problem whose sum comes as close to 100 as possible. This is not an "exact" game, so the sum can be more or less than 100. The player with the lower score wins the game.

Two-digit addition
Variation: Three-digit addition

Grade 3: CCSS.3.NBT.A.2
Grade 4: CCSS.4.NBT.B.4
Grade 5

Two players

Materials

- ten-frame cards with 10s removed, or standard deck with 10s and face cards removed
- paper
- pencils

How to play

The cards are shuffled and stacked facedown. Player 1 takes four cards and arranges the cards to create a two-digit addition problem whose sum will be as close to 100 as possible. Player 1 records the problem on his paper. Player 2 checks for addition accuracy. Player 2 takes four cards and does the same.

Example

Player 1 draws 8, 3, 4, and 1. He rearranges the cards until he decides that

$$
\begin{array}{r}
83 \\
+\ 14 \\
\hline
97
\end{array}
$$

is the closest he can get to 100. Player 2 checks Player 1's addition

Player 2 draws 5, 7, 2, and 7. She rearranges the cards and decides that

$$
\begin{array}{r}
75 \\
+\ 27 \\
\hline
102
\end{array}
$$

is the closest she can get to 100. Player 1 checks Player 2's addition.

The points for each round are the *difference* between the sum and 100.

In the example above, Player 1 scores three points, and Player 2 scores two points.

Players put their four cards in a discard pile. For the second round, Player 2 goes first. Players alternate starting positions after each round.

After six rounds, players total their points and the player with the lower score wins.

Questions

- Have you discovered a strategy that will help you get as close to 100 as possible?
- Why did you arrange your cards the way you did? Tell me what you are thinking.
- If you moved the cards around, could you make a problem whose sum is closer to 100?
- How did you figure out how close to 100 you are?

Variation: Modify the game to play "Get As Close as You Can to 1,000." Players take six cards to make a three-digit addition problem whose sum is as close to 1,000 as possible; otherwise, the game is played in the same way.

First One to 1,000 Wins!

The goal of the game is to be the first player to reach or pass 1,000.

Two-digit addition

Grade 3: CCSS.3.NBT.A.2
Grade 4: CCSS.4.NBT.B.4
Grade 5

Two players

Materials

- ten-frame cards with 10s removed, or standard deck with 10s and face cards removed

- paper

- pencils

How to play

The cards are shuffled and placed in a facedown stack.

Player 1 takes two cards. She makes the greatest two-digit number possible, and writes this number at the top of her paper. Player 2 takes two cards and proceeds in the same manner.

Player 1 takes two more cards. She again makes the greatest two-digit number possible and adds this number to the first number. Player 2 takes two more cards and does the same.

Players check each other's addition for accuracy.

Example

Player 1 takes 2 and 4. She makes 42, and writes it at the top of her paper. On her second turn, Player 1 draws 7 and 9 and makes 97. She adds 97 to her first number and finds the sum.

$$\begin{array}{r} 42 \\ + \ 97 \\ \hline 139 \end{array}$$

Player 2 checks Player 1's addition.

Players alternate turns until one player reaches or passes 1,000.

Questions

- What was your strategy for building the greatest two-digit number?
- Which numbers would you like to draw each time? Why?
- In building a number, which numbers would you put in your tens? Why?
- Which numbers would you put in your ones? Why?

Beat the Teacher

This is a group game that can be played by the whole class. The objective of this game is to get a sum greater than the teacher's or parent's sum.

Three-digit addition

Grade 3: CCSS.3.NBT.A.2
Grade 4: CCSS.4.NBT.B.4
Grade 5

Materials

- large die
- paper
- pencils

How to play

The teacher draws a large grid on the board (see below) for all to see. The children draw the same grid on their papers. (Grids may also be downloaded and printed, if desired.) The teacher also has a paper grid for his personal use. The game is played for a predetermined amount of time.

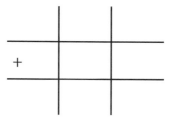

> Because this game may have a sum in the thousands, take time to explain that 13 hundreds, for example, can also be described as one thousand and three hundreds.

The teacher will roll the die a total of six times. Each time the die is rolled, the teacher calls out the number, and everyone must immediately write that number into any one of the spaces in the top two rows of the grid. Once written, the number cannot be moved to a different space. No numbers are entered in the bottom three spaces.

The teacher does the same on his paper grid but does not reveal his placement of the number to the class.

> I often check to make sure the children are immediately writing the number in a space. Also, if necessary, make them play the game with a pen or crayons so they are not tempted to move the number to a different space later in the game.

When all top six spaces have been filled, everyone completes the three-digit addition and places the sum in the bottom three spaces.

The teacher reveals his paper grid and fills the spaces of the grid on the board with his numbers and his sum. Students who have a sum that is greater than the teacher's sum "beat the teacher" and get two points.

Students who have a sum equal to the teacher's sum get one point.

At the end of the game session, the players with the most points are the winners.

When I introduce this game to a classroom of children, I don't tell them the goal of the game. I just tell them to put the rolled numbers anywhere they want in the top six spaces.

When everyone has done their addition, I tell them that to beat me they have to have a sum greater than mine. When the groan goes up from the students, I ask if there is something that they will do differently the next round, but I caution them not to tell me—just do it and see if it works.

Questions

Here are some questions to ask after the second round of play:

- What strategies have you discovered that will help you make a greater sum?

- Now that you know how the game is played, what will you do differently the next round?

- What did _____ [name of child] do differently that allowed her to have a greater sum than yours or the [adult]?

- Where is the best place to put a 9 if you want to make the greatest sum? Why?

- Where is the best place to put a 2 if you want to make the greatest sum? Why?

- Will you use the same strategies if you have to make a sum less than the [adult]?

- How likely were you to roll the _____ that you needed?

Variation: The game is played the same way, but the players with a sum less than the teacher's win two points.

It All Adds Up

Here's a way to play "Beat the Teacher" without the teacher! The object of this game is still to make the greatest sum possible.

Three-digit addition
Variations 1 & 2: Three-digit addition

Grade 3: CCSS.3.NBT.A.2
Grade 4: CCSS.4.NBT.B.4

Variation 3: Four-digit addition

Grade 4: CCSS.4.NBT.B.4
Grade 5

Two players

Materials

- ten-frame cards with 10s removed, or standard deck with 10s and face cards removed

- paper
- pencils

How to play

The game is played to a predetermined number of points to win. The players draw a grid like the one below. (Grids may also be downloaded and printed, if desired.)

> Because this game may have a sum in the thousands, take time to explain that 13 hundreds, for example, can also be described as one thousand and three hundreds.

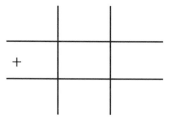

The cards are shuffled and placed facedown in a stack. Player 1 draws a card and places it faceup for both players to see. Each player writes this number in one of the spaces in the top two rows of his grid. Players keep their placement of the number a secret from each other. The number must be written down immediately. **Once written, it cannot be moved to a different space.** No numbers are placed in the bottom three spaces.

Player 2 draws a card and places it faceup for both players to see. The players select one of the remaining top five spaces on their grid and write the number in it.

Players continue to alternate taking a card until six cards have been turned over. When all top six spaces have been filled, players complete the three-digit addition, writing the sum in the bottom three spaces.

Players trade papers and check each other's addition. The player with the greater sum is the winner of that round and scores one point. The first player to reach the agreed upon score is the game winner.

Questions

• Have you discovered a strategy for placing your numbers that will give you the greatest sum?

• You have one space left. When the card is drawn, what number are you hoping it will be? How likely is it that it will be that number?

Variation 1: The game is played in the same manner, but the object of the game is to have the least sum.

Variation 2: While "It All Adds Up to 500" is played in the same way, players have to modify their strategies to create a sum that is as close as possible to 500 to win a round.

Variation 3: "Four-Digit It All Adds Up" is played in a similar manner, but each player takes eight cards to create a four-digit addition problem. See the sample grid below.

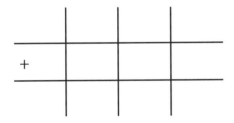

The Games

Rounding Numbers

Introduction

Rounding Basics 76

Rounding Glossary 76

Rounding to the Nearest Ten

Round Up (or Down)! 77

Target—200 78

Rounding to the Nearest Hundred

Rounded 80

Expert Rounding 82

Rounding to the Nearest Thousand

Rounded to Thousands 81

More Expert Rounding 83

Introduction

Rounding and estimation are important skills in math and in our daily lives. We round numbers all the time. Rounding numbers is used to give a precise estimate, but not an exact amount.

Rounding numbers is a crucial math skill. It makes numbers "friendly" and much easier to work with. Friendly numbers allow people to utilize the simplest multiplication, addition, subtraction, division, and counting patterns to make calculations and estimations. Using mental math to calculate the cost of 18 items @ $9.65 is far more complex than rounding $9.65 to $10 to get a rough number for the cost of the 18 items. There are obviously times when an exact number is necessary, but even in those instances, rounding is a good tool for checking the validity of your answer by giving you a ballpark figure.

Rounding Basics

In math, you can round up or round down. Rounding up happens when you have a value that is half or greater than the amount you are rounding to. Let's say you want to round to the nearest ten. If you were given the value 26, you would round up because 6 is greater than half of 10. If you were given 25, you would also round up. Rounding down is done when the value is less than half. Using a similar example, if you were given the number 24, you would round down because 4 is less than half of 10. Even if you were given the four-place decimal 24.9999, you would still round down because 4.9999 is less than 5 (half of 10).

The following games provide practice in rounding skills. For many children, a hundred chart might be helpful for visualizing the process of rounding.

Rounding Glossary

Rounding is changing a number to a more convenient or easily expressed value that is closely approximate to that of the original value. The process is often expressed as "rounding up," "rounding down," or "rounding off."

Round Up (or Down)!

The goal of this game is to cross off all the numbers on the game board.

Rounding to the nearest ten

Grade 3: CCSS.3.NBT.A.1
Grade 4: CCSS.4.NBT.A.3
Grade 5

Two players

Materials

- ten-frame cards with 0s and 10s removed, or standard deck with 10s and face cards removed

- pencils
- "Round Up (or Down)! game board for each player

10	20	30	40	50	60	70	80	90	100

How to play

The cards are shuffled and placed in a facedown stack. Player 1 takes two cards. He makes a two-digit number that when rounded to the nearest ten can be crossed off his game board. Player 1 puts the cards in a discard pile.

Example

Player 1 draws 1 and 7; he can make 17 or 71. He decides to make 71, rounds it to 70, and crosses off the 70 on his board.

Player 2 takes two cards and follows the same process.

Players alternate turns. If a player cannot make a number that can be crossed off the board, the player loses the turn. When the facedown cards have all been used, the discard pile is shuffled and placed facedown in a stack, and play continues.

The first player to cross off all the numbers on the game board wins.

> For many children, a hundred chart might be helpful for visualizing the process of rounding.

Questions

- Can you convince me that you have rounded to the nearest ten?
- What numbers would you need to cross off the _____? Anything else?

Target—200

The goal of this game is to have a sum as close to 200 as possible. Players must complete five full rounds of play. This is not an "exact" game, so the sum can be more or less than 200.

Two-digit addition

Grade 3: CCSS.3.NBT.A.2
Grade 4: CCSS.4.NBT.B.4
Grade 5

Two players

Materials

- ten-frame cards with 0s and 10s removed, or standard deck with 10s and face cards removed
- pencils
- "Target—200" recording sheet for each player

Round	Actual Number	Rounded Number
1		
2		
3		
4		
5		
	Sum	

How to play

The cards are shuffled and placed facedown in a stack.

Player 1 draws two cards and determines which two-digit number he wants to make. He then writes the number in the round 1 row under Actual Number. Player 1 rounds the actual number to the nearest ten and records it under Rounded Number. Player 1 puts his cards in a discard pile.

Example

Player 1 draws 4 and 7. He can make either 47 or 74, and decides to make 74. He writes 74 in the round 1 row under Actual Number, and then rounds it to 70, recording it under Rounded Number.

Round	Actual Number	Rounded Number
1	74	70

Player 2 draws two cards and proceeds in the same manner.

Players alternate turns until each has had five rounds of play. The player whose sum of rounded numbers comes closer to 200 wins the game.

Questions

- What did you discover while playing this game?

- Which strategies were helpful and which were not?

- Will you do the same thing next game or will you change your strategy?

- How did you figure out how far your sum is from 200?

- Can you prove to me that your sum is closer to 200 than the other player's?

Rounded

The goal of the game is to be the first player to fill in all the spaces on the recording sheet.

Rounding to the nearest hundred
Variation: Rounding to the nearest thousand

Grade 3: CCSS.3.NBT.A.1
Grade 4: CCSS.4.NBT.A.3
Grade 5

Two players

Materials

- ten-frame cards with 10s removed, or standard deck with 10s and face cards removed

- pencils

- "Rounded" recording sheet for each player

Rounded to	Actual Number
100	
200	
300	
400	
500	
600	
700	
800	
900	
1,000	

How to play

The cards are shuffled and placed facedown in a stack.

Player 1 takes three cards. She decides which three-digit number to make, and then determines the correct rounded hundred line on which to write the actual number. Player 1 puts the cards in a discard pile.

Example

Player 1 draws 4, 7, and 9, which can be arranged as 479, 497, 749, 794, 947, or 974. She decides to make 794 and writes it on the 800 line.

Player 2 takes three cards and proceeds in the same manner.

If a player cannot use any combination of three numbers because those lines are already filled, that player loses a turn.

Players alternate turns. When the facedown cards have all been used, the discard pile is shuffled and stacked facedown. Play continues until one of the players completely fills in her game board, winning the game.

Questions

- Is there another way you can rearrange those three numbers so that you can create a three-digit number that will fit in an empty space on your recording sheet?

- Can you prove to me that _____ is rounded to _____?

- What are some three-digit numbers that could be rounded to _____? Anything else?

Variation: "Rounded to Thousands" is played in a similar manner, but the game and recording sheet are modified so that players take four cards to create a four-digit number that is rounded to the nearest thousand.

Expert Rounding

The object of this game is to round three-digit numbers to the nearest ten and hundred.

Rounding to the nearest ten and hundred
Variation: Rounding to the nearest ten, hundred, and thousand

Grade 3: CCSS.3.NBT.A.1
Grade 4: CCSS.4.NBT.A.3
Grade 5

Two players

Materials

- ten-frame cards with 0s and 10s removed, or standard deck with 10s and face cards removed

- pencils

- "Expert Rounding" recording sheet for each player

Round	Actual Number	Rounded to Nearest Ten	Rounded to Nearest Hundred
1			
2			
3			
4			
5			
6			
7			
8			
9			
10			

How to play

The cards are shuffled and placed in a facedown stack. Player 1 takes three cards and determines which three-digit number to make. He verbalizes the number and then proceeds as follows:

Rounds the actual number to the nearest ten.

Rounds the actual number to the nearest hundred.

Writes the actual and rounded numbers on the recording sheet.

Example: Player 1 draws the 2, 8, and 5 cards. He decides to make 582.

Round	Actual Number	Number rounded to nearest ten	Number rounded to nearest hundred
1	582	580	600

Player 1 puts his cards in a discard pile.

Player 2 checks Player 1's recording sheet for accuracy. Players with correct answers score one point. Player 1 earns one point.

Player 2 draws three cards and proceeds in the same manner.

When the facedown cards have all been used, the discard pile is shuffled and stacked facedown.

At the end of ten rounds, the player with more points wins the game.

Variation: "More Expert Rounding" is played in a similar manner, but the game and recording sheet are modified so that players take four cards and round to the nearest ten, hundred, and thousand.

The Games

Subtraction

Introduction

Subtraction Glossary 86

Subtracting a One-Digit Number from a One-Digit Number

Simple Subtraction 87

More: A Game of Differences 89

Subtraction Ladder 91

Four-in-a-Row Subtraction 93

Subtracting a One-Digit Number from a Two-Digit Number

Lesser Difference Subtraction 95

100 Going Down (or Up)! 97

Subtracting a Two-Digit Number from a Two-Digit Number

Double-Digit Game of Differences 90

Double Subtraction 99

Make a Difference 101

Subtracting a Two-Digit Number from a Three-Digit Number

500 Going Down (or Up)! 103

Begin with 1,000 105

Subtracting a Three-Digit Number from a Three-Digit Number

Triple-Digit Subtraction 100

Beat-the-Teacher Subtraction. 107

Creating and Comparing Differences. 109

Subtracting a Three-Digit Number from a Four-Digit Number

5,000 Going Down (or Up)! 104

Agree on a Difference. 111

Subtracting a Four-Digit Number from a Four-Digit Number

Four-Digit Subtraction 100

Introduction

Math can be compared to a table with four legs: addition, subtraction, multiplication, and division. As with any table, when one leg is faulty or breaks, that table is of little use, if any. Similarly, without a thorough understanding of subtraction, children won't have a sturdy foundation on which to develop more complex math abilities.

Subtraction is taking a number or a quantity away from another number or quantity, and this concept can be perplexing for children. Part of the challenge for children lies in the fact that subtraction is often taught by starting with abstract ideas—24 minus 9 equals 15. Children's difficulties with subtraction illustrate the necessity of first teaching the concept with objects or manipulatives and connecting their subtraction experiences to concrete, real-life situations. For example, have students count out 24 pennies, "take away" 9, and count how many are left. Counting out objects and then taking away a designated quantity allows children to visually see the difference. If children are not given opportunities to make these connections, then they have to resort to learning by rote. Using real, physical objects to instruct difficult concepts supports children's learning by connecting the ideas to what they can see and know, and thus the learning becomes more secure and more useful.

When posed with a subtraction math fact, another efficient way to solve it is by knowing the related addition fact, for example, $7 + 8 = 15$ and $15 - 7 = 8$. When the recall of addition facts is automatic and students understand the connection between addition and subtraction facts, their fluency with subtraction facts naturally increases.

To attain fluency with subtraction facts, children need ongoing opportunities to practice them—something the following games will provide—and with that, the games will also help develop students' understanding of subtraction.

Subtraction Glossary

When playing any math games, it is important that the children become familiar with the correct math terminology for certain facts and concepts. In this section there are four words that should be introduced and consistently used; their definitions are below.

Digit is a symbol (numeral) used to indicate a numeric value. For example, 5 is a one-digit number, 15 is a two-digit number, and 150 is a three-digit number.

Difference is the amount by which two numbers differ in quantity. It is also the answer to a subtraction problem.

minuend		subtrahend		difference
10	−	5	=	5

Equal is having the same amount or identical value.

Equation, sometimes called a number sentence, is a mathematical statement that contains an equals sign, indicating that the two expressions are equal.

$$10 - 5 = 5$$
$$5 = 10 - 5$$
$$9 - 4 = 10 - 5$$

Simple Subtraction

The goal of this game is to have the smallest difference.

One-digit subtraction
Comparing differences

Grade 3: CCSS.3.NBT.A2

Two players

Materials

- ten-frame cards, or standard deck with face cards removed
- "Simple Subtraction" recording sheet

	Player 1		Player 2
Turn	Equation (number sentence)	> = <	Equation (number sentence)
1	– =		=
2	– =		=
3	– =		=
4	– =		=
5	– =		=

How to play

The cards are shuffled and placed facedown in a stack. Player 1 takes two cards. She subtracts the smaller number from the greater number. Player 2 turns over two cards and does the same. The player with the smallest difference wins all four cards.

In the event of a tie, that is, both players have the same difference, each player takes two more cards and subtracts the smaller number from the greater number. The player with the smaller difference wins all eight cards.

Example

Player 1 draws 4 and 7. She subtracts the 4 from the 7 to get a difference of 3. Player 2 draws 9 and 8. He subtracts the 8 from the 9 to get a difference of 1. Player 2 wins the round and takes all four cards because a difference of 1 is less than a difference of 3.

Players write their equations on the recording sheet and work together to decide which symbol—greater than, less than, or equal to—should be used.

Turn	Player 1 Equation	> = <	Player 2 Equation
1	7 – 4 = 3	>	9 – 8 = 1

Players alternate turns until all the cards in the facedown stack have been used. Players count their cards. The winner is the player with more or fewer (you decide) cards.

Questions

- How did you figure out the difference between your two numbers?
- If your goal is to make the smallest difference, what kind of numbers are you looking for?
- If your goal is making the greatest difference, what kind of numbers are you looking for?

Variation: The game is played in the same way but the player with the greatest difference takes all four cards.

More: A Game of Differences

The goal of this game is to have more counters than the other player.

One-digit subtraction
Variation: Two-digit subtraction

Grade 3: CCSS.3.NBT.A2
Grade 4: CCSS.4.NBT.B.4
Grade 5

Two players

Materials

- ten-frame cards, or a standard deck with face cards removed

- counters

How to play

The cards are shuffled and stacked facedown. Each player turns over one card. Players decide who has the greater number, and then figure out how much more that player has. The player who has more takes the quantity of counters that equals the difference between the two players' numbers. The used cards are placed in a discard pile.

Example

Player 1 turns over a 3. Player 2 turns over a 9. Player 2 has the greater number, which is six more than Player 1's, so Player 2 takes six counters.

Play continues until all the cards in the facedown stack have been used. Players count their counters, and the player with more counters wins the game.

> As the children become more adept at the game, it is important that each player begins to record the equation for each turn on a sheet of paper. If Player 1 has 3 and Player 2 has 9, the equation would be $9 - 3 = 6$. This transforms the thought process and action to a written record of what those tasks actually look like in terms of an equation.

Questions

- How did you figure out how much more you had? What did you do?

- Can you convince me that _____ is that much more than _____?

- When you take a lot of counters in a turn, what do you notice about the two numbers drawn?

- What do you notice about the amount of counters you get when both numbers are close to each other?

Variation: Each player turns over two cards and makes the greatest two-digit number possible in "Double-Digit Game of Differences." The players then determine who has the greater number and, using pencil and paper, figure out the difference between the two numbers. The player who has the greater difference gives himself points equal to the difference between the two numbers. After all the facedown cards have been used, players count their points. The player with more points wins the game.

Example

Player 1 draws a 6 and a 7, and makes 76. Player 2 draws a 1 and a 3, and makes 31. Player 1 has the greater number, in this case 45 more, so Player 1 scores 45 points for this round.

The Games

Subtraction Ladder

The goal of this game is to create subtraction equations that allow a player to put an equation on each rung of the ladder.

One-digit subtraction

Grade 3: CCSS.3.NBT.A2

Grade 4

Grade 5

Two players

Materials

- ten-frame cards, or a standard deck with face cards removed
- paper
- pencils

How to play

Each player draws a ladder with nine rungs on his sheet of paper. (Ladders may also be downloaded and printed, if desired.)

	= 9
	= 8
	= 7
	= 6
	= 5
	= 4
	= 3
	= 2
	= 1

The cards are shuffled and placed facedown in a stack. Player 1 takes five cards and puts them faceup in a line.

Player 1 uses two of these cards to make one side of an equation that has a difference between 1 and 9, and writes it on the appropriate rung of his ladder.

Example

Player 1 draws 5, 9, 1, 3, and 3. Player 1 decides to make 9 – 5 and writes it on the 4 rung of his ladder.

	= 9
	= 8
	= 7
	= 6
	= 5
9 – 5	= 4
	= 3
	= 2
	= 1

Player 1 puts the two used cards in a discard pile.

Player 2 draws five cards and puts them faceup in a line and proceeds in the same manner.

Players can put only one equation on each line. If a player cannot make an equation, that player picks two cards from her line to put in the discard pile, and loses that turn.

Before taking their next turn, the players draw two more cards from the facedown stack so that they always have five cards to work with.

Players alternate turns until one player wins by filling in all nine rungs on her ladder.

If the cards in the facedown stack run out, the discard pile is shuffled, stacked facedown, and play continues.

Questions

- What did you discover while playing this game?

- Were there any differences that were more difficult to make? Why?

- What equations could you use that would equal ____?

- What strategy might you try in the next game?

Four-in-a-Row Subtraction

This game generates a lot of mental subtraction practice. Its goal is to have four counters in a vertical, horizontal, or diagonal row.

One-digit subtraction

Grade 3: CCSS.3.NBT.A2

Grade 4

Grade 5

Two players

Materials

- two paper clips

- different counters for each player

- "Four-in-a-Row Subtraction" game board

7	2	4	3	6
3	5	0	7	8
1	0	5	6	9
2	8	6	4	7
4	5	3	1	8

0	1	2	3	4	5	6	7	8	9

Player 1 places two paper clips under any two of the numbers in the line below the game grid. The two paper clips can be placed under the same number.

Player 1 subtracts the smaller number from the greater number and places one of her counters on one of the corresponding differences on the game grid.

From this point on, only one paper clip can be moved.

Player 2 moves one paper clip under a new number. He subtracts the smaller number from the greater number, and places a counter on that difference.

Example

Player 1 places one paper clip under the 4 and the other under the 2. She subtracts 4 – 2, and places a counter on one of the 2s in the grid.

Player 2 leaves one paper clip on the 2 and moves the other paper clip to the 9. He subtracts 9 – 2, and puts one of his counters on one of the 7s in the grid.

If a difference already has a counter on it, another counter may not be put on top.

Players alternate turns in this manner until one player has four counters in a vertical, horizontal, or diagonal row.

When I introduce this game at school, I play it with the whole class. I use a document camera to project the game board, including the number line.

I divide the class in half and the left side of the room (red) plays against the right side of the room (blue). I have found that round transparent counters, available at many education supply stores, work best. (I'm often asked how I decide which team goes first. There are many possibilities. I always respond, "This is no longer my game. It's yours. You decide. Do what works best for your children.")

One team begins the game by telling me where to put the two paper clips. Almost always, I take the first suggestion I hear. The suggestion maker must give me a full equation; for instance, "Put the first paper clip under the four and the second under the six. Six minus four equals two." So I put that team's counter on the 2 in the grid to which they direct me.

It's now the other team's turn, but they can move only one paper clip. Again, I take the first suggestion I hear.

At some point, the students on both teams begin to disagree about which paper clip should be moved. I give them about a minute to get organized, talk about possible strategies, and decide how they are going to proceed.

Once the game is learned, I put them in pairs, and they play against each other with paper copies of the game board, counters, and two paper clips.

Questions

- After looking at the counters already on the board, which differences would be helpful because they would get another counter on the board in addition to one you already have?

- Which numbers might you use to get that difference? Anything else?

- Which differences would help you block the other player from getting four in a row?

Lesser Difference Subtraction

The goal of this game is to have the lesser difference.

One-digit subtraction from a two-digit number

Grade 3: CCSS.3.NBT.A.2
Grade 4: CCSS.4.NBT.B.4
Grade 5

Two players

Materials

- ten-frame cards, or a standard deck with face cards removed
- paper
- pencils

How to play

The cards are shuffled and stacked facedown.

Player 1 takes three cards and makes a two-digit number with two of the cards. He then subtracts the remaining number from the two-digit one. Player 2 takes three cards and proceeds in the same manner.

Example

Player 1 takes a 7, 5, and 4, and creates this problem:

$$
\begin{array}{r}
45 \\
-\ 7 \\
\hline
38
\end{array}
$$

Player 2 draws a 9, 6, and 2, and creates this problem:

$$
\begin{array}{r}
26 \\
-\ 9 \\
\hline
17
\end{array}
$$

Players check each other's subtraction for accuracy and compare the resulting differences. The player with the lesser difference wins a point. (In the example above, Player 2 wins the point for that round.) Play continues until one player has ten points.

Questions

- What did you discover while playing this game?

- What strategies helped you have the least possible difference?

- Why did you arrange your numbers the way you did?

- Could you arrange your numbers any differently and get a smaller difference?

Variation: Play the same game, but the winner of the point is the player whose difference is greater.

100 Going Down (or Up)!

The goal of this game is to be the first player to reach or pass 0.

One-digit subtraction from 100

Grade 3: CCSS.3.NBT.A.2
Grade 4: CCSS.4.NBT.B.4
Grade 5

Two players

Materials

- die
- paper
- pencils

How to play

Players start with 100 points, and write 100 at the top of their papers. Player 1 rolls the die and subtracts that number from 100. Player 2 checks Player 1's subtraction for accuracy and initials it if correct.

Example

Player 1 rolls a 4 and, writing on his paper, subtracts 4 from 100:

> 100
> − 4
> 96

Player 2 checks Player 1's subtraction and initials it.

Player 2 takes her turn, and play proceeds in the same manner, with players alternating turns and checking each other's subtraction.

> There's only one complication! Whenever a 6 is rolled, the rules change. Players don't subtract. Instead, they add 6 to their total.

Example

Player 2 rolls a 6 and she writes on her paper:

> *100*
> *+ 6*
> *106*

Player 1 checks her addition and initials it.

The first player to reach or pass 0 wins the game.

Questions

- What have you noticed about playing this game?
- If you want to reach zero first, what are the best numbers to roll?

The Games

Double Subtraction

The object of this game is to make two-digit subtraction problems that result in the smallest possible differences.

Two-digit subtraction

Grade 3: CCSS.3.NBT.A.2
Grade 4: CCSS.4.NBT.B.4
Grade 5

Variation 1: Three-digit subtraction
Variation 2: Four-digit subtraction

Two players

Materials

- ten-frame cards with 10s removed, or standard deck with 10s and face cards removed

- paper

- pencils

How to play

The cards are shuffled and put facedown in a stack.

Player 1 takes four cards and arranges them to make a two-digit subtraction problem that will have the smallest possible difference. Player 2 checks Player 1's subtraction for accuracy and initials it if correct. Player 1 places her four cards in a discard pile.

Example

Player 1 draws 7, 5, 1, and 8. She rearranges the cards, and decides to make 81 and 75. She writes down on her paper:

$$\begin{array}{r} 81 \\ -\ \underline{75} \\ 6 \end{array}$$

Player 2 checks Player 1's subtraction and initials it.

Player 2 takes four cards and play proceeds in the same manner. The players then compare their results. The player with the smaller difference scores one point.

Players alternate turns. When all the cards in the facedown stack have been used, the discard pile is shuffled, stacked facedown, and play continues. The first player to score ten points is the winner.

Questions

- Why did you decide to arrange your numbers the way you did?

- Could you arrange your numbers any differently and make a smaller difference?

- How did you figure out what the difference is between your two two-digit numbers?

- Have you discovered a strategy that helps you arrange your numbers to make the smallest difference?

- Would this strategy work if you were trying to make the greatest difference?

Variation 1: To play "Triple-Digit Subtraction," the game is modified so that each player draws six cards to make three-digit subtraction problems that have the smallest differences possible.

Variation 2: To play "Four-Digit Subtraction," the game is modified so that each player draws eight cards to make four-digit subtraction problems that have the smallest differences possible.

Make a Difference

The goal of the game is to have the greatest difference.

Two-digit subtraction

Grade 3: CCSS.3.NBT.A.2
Grade 4: CCSS.4.NBT.B.4
Grade 5

Two players

Materials

- die
- two counters for each player
- paper
- pencils
- "Make a Difference" game board for each player

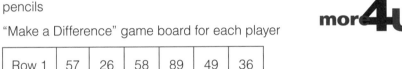

Row 1	57	26	58	89	49	36
Row 2	52	23	48	10	77	47
Row 3	56	38	25	61	20	70
Row 4	66	41	91	39	80	54
Row 5	75	12	74	64	86	90
Row 6	17	53	20	33	79	55

How to play

Player 1 rolls the die and selects a number from that row on the game board and puts a counter on it. Player 2 rolls the die and proceeds in the same manner.

Player 1 rolls the die a second time and puts his second counter on a number in that row. (If a player's second roll is the same as his first, both numbers must be selected from the same row.) Player 2 rolls the die a second time and puts her second counter on a number in that row.

Example

Player 1 rolls a 3 and puts his counter on any number in Row 3. On his second roll, Player 1 again rolls a 3. He puts his counter on another number in Row 3.

Subtraction

Player 1 sets up his two-digit subtraction problem on a sheet of paper using the two numbers marked with his counters and finds the difference between the two numbers. Player 2 checks his subtraction for accuracy and initials the work if it is correct.

Player 2 sets up her two-digit subtraction problem and finds the difference between the two numbers. Player 1 checks Player 2's subtraction for accuracy and initials the work if it is correct. Play proceeds in the same manner. Players compare their subtraction differences. The player with the greater difference earns a point for that round. The first player to earn ten points wins the game.

Questions

- Did you find a strategy for picking numbers that will give you the greater difference?
- Would that same strategy work if you were trying to find the smaller difference? See what happens when you play the variation.

Variation: Play the game exactly the same way, but the player with the lesser difference wins.

500 Going Down (or Up)!

The first player to reach or pass 0 wins the game.

Two-digit subtraction from 500
Variation: Three-digit subtraction from 5,000

Grade 3: CCSS.3.NBT.A.2
Grade 4: CCSS.4.NBT.B.4
Grade 5

Two players

Materials

- two dice
- paper
- pencils

How to play

Players start with 500 points, and write 500 at the top of their papers.

Player 1 rolls the dice, and he makes a two-digit number, and then subtracts that number from 500. Player 2 checks Player 1's subtraction for accuracy and initials it if correct.

Example

Player 1 rolls a 2 and 4. He can make 24 or 42. He decides to make 42 and, writing on his paper, subtracts 42 from 500.

```
  500
 - 42
  458
```

Player 2 checks his subtraction and initials it.

Player 2 takes her turn, and play proceeds in the same manner, with players alternating turns and checking each other's subtraction.

> There's only one complication! Whenever a 1 is rolled, the rules change. Players don't subtract. Instead, they make a two-digit number and add that number to their total.

Example

Player 1 rolls a 1 and a 5. He can make 15 or 51. He decides to make 15, and then adds it to his previous total.

    458
  + 15
    473

The first person to reach or pass 0 wins.

> Be careful not to give children any hints or tips as to which two-digit number to create when subtracting or adding. Let them discover the number for themselves through the questions you ask.

Questions

- Did you discover any helpful strategies for subtracting and adding in this game?
- If you are subtracting, how did you decide which two-digit number to use?
- Will you use that same strategy if you have to add? Why or why not?

Variation: To play "5,000 Going Down (or Up)!," the game is modified so that players start with 5,000 points and roll three dice to create a three-digit number to subtract from their total. If a 1 is rolled, the three-digit number is added to the total. The first person to reach or pass 0 wins the game.

Begin with 1,000

Each player starts with 1,000 points. The goal of the game is to be the first player to reach or pass 0.

Two-digit subtraction from 1,000

Grade 3: CCSS.3.NBT.A.2
Grade 4: CCSS.4.NBT.B.4
Grade 5

Two players

Materials

- ten-frame cards with 10s removed, or standard deck with 10s and face cards removed

- paper
- pencils

How to play

The cards are shuffled and stacked facedown. Players write 1000 at the top of their papers.

Player 1 draws two cards and decides which two-digit number to make. He subtracts it from 1,000. Player 2 checks Player 1's subtraction and initials it if correct. Player 1 places his two cards in a discard pile.

Example

Player 1 turns over a 9 and a 3. She can make either 39 or 93 and subtract it from 1,000. She writes on her paper:

> 1,000
> − 93
> ——
> 907

Player 2 checks Player 1's subtraction and initials it.

Player 2 turns over two cards and proceeds in the same manner.

Players alternate turns. When all the cards in the facedown stack have been used, the discard pile is shuffled, stacked facedown, and play continues. The first player to reach or pass 0 wins.

> Be careful not to give the children any hints or tips as to which two-digit number to create when subtracting. Let them discover it for themselves through questions you ask.

Questions

- Did you find a strategy that helped you when subtracting?

- Since you are subtracting, how did you decide which two-digit number to use?

Beat-the-Teacher Subtraction

This is a group game that can be played by the whole class. The objective of this game is to get a difference less than the teacher's or parent's difference.

Three-digit subtraction

Grade 3: CCSS.3.NBT.A.2
Grade 4: CCSS.4.NBT.B.4
Grade 5

Materials

* one large die
* paper
* pencils

How to play

The teacher draws a large grid on the board (see below) for all to see. The children draw the same grid on their papers. (Grids may also be downloaded and printed, if desired.) The teacher also has a paper grid for her personal use. The game is played for a predetermined amount of time. The die will be rolled a total of six times by the parent or teacher.

Each time the die is rolled, the teacher calls out the number, and the children must immediately put the number into any one of the six spaces of the top two rows on the grid. **Once written, the number cannot be moved to a different space**. Numbers cannot be placed in the bottom three spaces.

The teacher does the same on her paper grid but does not reveal her placement of the number to the class.

> I often check to make sure the children are immediately writing the number in a space. Also, you might consider making them play the game with a pen or crayons so they are not tempted to move the number to a different space later in the game.

The die is rolled five more times. When all top six spaces have been filled, everyone completes the subtraction and places the difference in the bottom three spaces. Players trade papers and check each other's addition for accuracy.

The teacher reveals her paper grid and fills the spaces of the grid on the board with her numbers and her difference. Students who have a difference that is less than the teacher's difference "beat the teacher" and get two points. Students who have a difference equal to the teacher's get one point.

At the end of the game session, the players with the most points are the winners.

> For children who have not yet dealt with negative numbers, if the larger number ends up on the second row of the grid (the "bottom" of the subtraction problem), that player is out of that round and gets no points. If children have dealt with negative numbers, then by all means, let them try creating problems with negative outcomes. The strategies for placing numbers for negative outcomes are completely different and should be discussed.

Questions

- What strategies have you discovered that will help you to make the least possible difference?
- What did (name of child) do differently that allowed him to have a difference less than the teacher's?
- Will you use the same strategies if you have to make a difference greater than the teacher's?
- How likely was it that the _____ you needed would be rolled?

Variation: The game is played the same way, but the players with a difference greater than the teacher's win two points.

Creating and Comparing Differences

Here's a way to play "Beat the Teacher Subtraction" without the teacher! The object of this game is still to make the smallest difference possible.

Three-digit subtraction

Grade 3: CCSS.3.NBT.A.2
Grade 4: CCSS.4.NBT.B.4
Grade 5

Two players

Materials

- ten-frame cards with 10s removed, or standard deck with 10s and face cards removed

- paper

- pencils

How to play

The game is played for a fixed period of time. Players make a grid on their sheets of paper for each round. (Grids may also be downloaded and printed, if desired.)

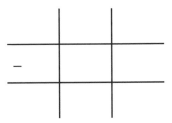

The cards are shuffled and placed facedown in a stack. Player 1 draws a card that is placed faceup for both players to see. Each player writes this number in one of the six spaces of the top two rows on his grid. The number must be written down immediately. **Once written, it cannot be moved to a different space**. Numbers cannot be placed in the bottom three spaces.

Player 2 draws a second card that is placed faceup for both players to see. The player selects one of the remaining top five spaces on his grid and writes the number of the card in it.

Players alternate drawing a card until six cards have been turned over and the numbers written in each player's grid. When all six top spaces have been filled in, players complete the subtraction, writing the difference in the bottom three spaces.

Players exchange papers and check each other's subtraction for accuracy. The player with the smaller difference is the winner for that round and scores one point. In the event of a tie, each player receives a point. At the end of the game period, the player with more points wins the game.

For children who have not yet dealt with negative numbers, if the larger number ends up on the second row of the grid (the "bottom" of the subtraction problem), that player is out of that round and gets no points.

If children have dealt with negative numbers, then by all means, let them try creating problems with negative differences. The strategies for placing numbers for negative outcomes are completely different and should be discussed.

Questions

- What strategies have you discovered that will help you make the least possible difference?

- What did (name of child) do differently that allowed her to have a difference less than yours?

- How likely were you to draw the ____ that you needed?

Variation: The game is played in the same way, but the player with the greatest difference wins the round.

Agree on a Difference

The object of this game is to subtract a three-digit number from a four-digit number.

Three-digit subtraction

Grade 3: CCSS.3.NBT.A.2
Grade 4: CCSS.4.NBT.B.4
Grade 5

Two players

Materials

- ten-frame cards with 0s and 10s removed, or standard deck with 10s and face cards removed

- paper

- pencils

How to play

The cards are shuffled and stacked facedown.

Player 1 takes four cards. She arranges the cards to create the *least* possible four-digit number.

Player 2 takes three cards. He arranges them to make the *greatest* possible three-digit number.

Both players subtract the three-digit number from the four-digit number and find the difference.

Example

Player 1 draws 6, 2, 7, and 1. She makes 1,267. Player 2 draws 5, 8, and 2. He makes 852. Both players set up the same problem on their sheets of paper:

```
  1267
-  852
   415
```

Players with the correct difference earn one point. (If both players have the correct difference, both get a point.)

If the players don't agree on the difference, they check each other's work to find the error. Only the player whose difference was originally correct gets a point.

The used cards are placed in a discard pile.

Players alternate roles building four- and three-digit numbers until all the cards have been used. The player with more points is the winner of the game.

Questions

- What did you discover while playing this game?

- What was easy about this game? What was more difficult?

The Games

Multiplication

Introduction

    Multiplication Glossary 114

One-Digit Multiplication

    Circles and Triangles 115

    Count the Points 117

    Rectangles 119

    Constant Factor Multiplication 121

    Multiplication War 123

    Reverse Multiplication Bingo 125

    Multiplication Lotto 127

    Multiplication Block It 129

    Salute Multiplication 131

    Multiplication Bingo 132

    Multiplication Unscramble 134

    Factor Hunt 136

Multiplying a Two-Digit Number by a One-Digit Number

    Multiple Multiplication 138

    Going for the Greatest 140

    Multiplication Beat the Teacher 141

    Strategy Multiplication 143

    Target—300 145

    Move-It-Around Multiplication 147

Multiplying a Two-Digit Number by a Two-Digit Number

    Double-Digit Multiplication Beat the Teacher 142

    Two-Digit Strategy Multiplication 144

    More Move-It-Around Multiplication 147

Multiplying a Three-Digit Number by a Two-Digit Number

    Multidigit Multiplication Beat the Teacher 142

    Multidigit Strategy Multiplication 144

Introduction

We use multiplication frequently in our daily lives. Understanding the concepts of multiplication and memorizing multiplication facts are two important rungs on the mathematics ladder. If children fail to master either step, they will find that division, long multiplication, fractions, and algebra will be much more difficult than they should be, and some children may very well begin to lose confidence.

Students first need to understand that multiplication can be considered in different ways: It is the grouping of sets, repeated addition, and a faster way of adding. However, there eventually comes a time when the importance of rapid recall needs to be highlighted. Students have to be aware that they must recall the product instantly.

Memorizing the multiplication facts is facilitated by the following games. Focus your limited time on the facts that need to be learned. If you skip the facts the children already know and if they have learned the reciprocal facts together (e.g., 6 x 7 and 7 x 6), there are surprisingly few left to memorize. Review all facts occasionally to make sure they have been retained in long-term memory. Games can help with retention.

Multiplication Glossary

When playing any math games, it is important that the children become familiar with the correct math terminology for certain facts and concepts. In this section there are three words that should be introduced and consistently used; their definitions are below.

Factor is a whole number that is multiplied with another number (factor) to make a third number (product).

Product is the amount realized when two (or more) factors are multiplied together; the answer to a multiplication problem.

$$\begin{array}{ccccc} \text{factor} & & \text{factor} & \text{equals} & \text{product} \\ 3 & \times & 3 & = & 9 \end{array}$$

Exponent is a small number placed upper right of a base number that indicates the number of times the base number is multiplied by itself.

$$5^3 \ (5 \times 5 \times 5 = 125)$$

Circles and Triangles

This game is a very concrete depiction of multiplication. Its goal is to make equal groups.

One-digit multiplication

Grade 3: CCSS.3.OA.C.7
Grade 4: CCSS.4.NBT.B.5

Two players

Materials

- ten-frame cards 1–6, four of each; the same if using standard deck
- pencils
- "Circles and Triangles" recording sheet for each player

Round 1	Round 2
____ circles × ____triangles in each circle = ____triangles	____ circles × ____triangles in each circle = ____triangles
Round 3	Round 4
____ circles × ____triangles in each circle = ____triangles	____ circles × ____triangles in each circle = ____triangles

How to play

The cards are shuffled and placed facedown in a stack. Player 1 takes a card and draws that number of circles in the round 1 box on his recording sheet. Player 2 takes a card and proceeds in the same manner.

Player 1 takes a second card and puts that number of triangles inside each circle. Player 2 takes a second card and proceeds in the same manner.

Example

Player 1 takes a 5 for his first card and draws five circles in the Round 1 box. For his second card, Player 1 gets a 3. He draws three triangles inside each circle.

Each player records a multiplication equation that reflects—

- how many circles were drawn;
- how many triangles were put in each circle; and
- how many triangles are in all of the circles.

Players read their equations to each other and check for accuracy.

Player 1 draws the fifth card of the round.

If the card is an *odd* number, the player with more triangles wins the round. If the card is an *even* number, the player with fewer triangles wins the round.

The five used cards are put in a discard pile. When the facedown cards have all been used, the discard pile is shuffled, stacked facedown, and play continues.

The players alternate drawing first to start each round, that is, Player 2 starts round 2 by taking the first card; Player 1 starts round 3 by taking the first card, and so on.

Questions

- Why did you end up with more (or less) than the other player?

- Can you explain to me why ____ × ____ = ____? Could you show it in a different way?

- What factor would have given you more (or less) than the other player?

Variations: As the children get more familiar with the game, it can be modified by adding the 7s, then 8s, and so forth, to the card deck.

The Games

Count the Points

This game offers a concrete representation of multiplication.

One-digit multiplication

Grade 3: CCSS.3.OA.C.7
Grade 4: CCSS.4.NBT.B.5

Two players

Materials

- ten-frame cards 1–5, four of each; the same if using standard deck

- paper

- pencils

- "Count the Points" recording sheet for each player

Round	Equations
1	___ vertical lines × ___ horizontal lines = ___ points of intersection (product)
2	___ vertical lines × ___ horizontal lines = ___ points of intersection (product)
3	___ vertical lines × ___ horizontal lines = ___ points of intersection (product)
4	___ vertical lines × ___ horizontal lines = ___ points of intersection (product)
5	___ vertical lines × ___ horizontal lines = ___ points of intersection (product)
6	___ vertical lines × ___ horizontal lines = ___ points of intersection (product)
	Sum of products ___

How to play

The cards are shuffled and placed facedown in a stack. Player 1 takes a card and draws the number of vertical lines indicated by the card. Player 2 takes a card and does the same.

Player 1 takes a second card and draws the number of horizontal lines indicated, crisscrossing the vertical lines. Player 2 takes a card and does the same. Both players then highlight the points of intersection between the two sets of lines. Each player records the multiplication equation under the grid. This product is recorded as the player's score for that round.

Example

Player 1 turns over a 4 for his first card and draws four vertical lines.

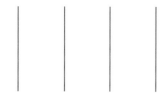

For his second card, Player 1 turns over a 3 and draws three horizontal lines crisscrossing the vertical lines.

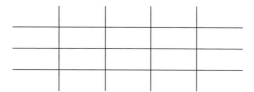

Player 1 highlights the points of intersection between the two sets of lines on his paper. He has three rows with four points in each row, and writes the equation, 3 x 4 = 12. He scores twelve points for this round.

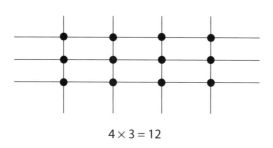

$$4 \times 3 = 12$$

The play continues with players alternating turns. After six rounds, players add the products for each round. The player with the greater sum wins the game.

This is a great strategy for helping children calculate multiplication problems fairly quickly. I find that students often create this grid when they don't know the answer to a specific multiplication problem.

Questions

- Why does this work?

- Is there another way to create a picture of ____?

- Will this work for every multiplication problem?

Variation: The game is played in the same way, but using cards 1 to 10, four of each.

Rectangles

Players roll two dice whose numbers determine the length and width of rectangles that are then drawn on a 12 by 12 grid. Players score points by finding the areas of the rectangles.

One-digit multiplication

Grade 3: CCSS.3.OA.C.7
Grade 4: CCSS.4.NBT.B.5
Grade 5

Two players

Materials

- two dice
- pencils
- crayons

- "Rectangles" 12 by 12 grid for each player

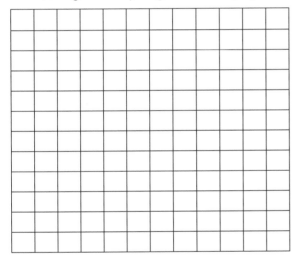

How to play

The rules for drawing the rectangles are explained to the players:

- All rectangles must be placed entirely within the 12 by 12 grid.
- The edges of rectangles may touch, but they do not have to.
- Rectangles may not overlap each other.
- No rectangle may be placed inside another rectangle.

Player 1 rolls the dice and draws a rectangle by marking its width in pencil on a horizontal line on the grid according to the number thrown on one die, and marking its length according to the number thrown on the other die.

Example

Player 1 rolls a 4 and 5. Player 1 draws a 4 x 5 rectangle anywhere on the grid.

The player then—

* outlines the entire rectangle;

* calculates his score by determining the number of squares within the rectangle;

* writes the entire equation within that rectangle (e.g., 4 x 5 = 20); and

* colors it in.

Player 2 rolls the dice and proceeds in the same manner.

When the roll of the dice results in a rectangle that will not fit on a player's grid, the player drops out of the game and calculates her cumulative score.

The game ends when both players can no longer draw a rectangle that will fit on their grids. The player with the highest score wins.

Questions

* What did you discover while playing this game?

* When you play it a second time, will you do anything differently?

* Is it better to roll numbers that are greater or smaller? Why or why not?

Constant Factor Multiplication

The goal of this game is to have the greatest product.

One-digit multiplication

Grade 3: CCSS.3.OA.C.7
Grade 4: CCSS.4.NBT.B.5
Grade 5 Two players

Materials

- ten-frame cards 1–5, four of each; the same if using standard deck

How to play

Players sit side by side. The multiplication fact to practice is chosen and one card with that factor (number) is placed between the two players. The cards are shuffled and stacked facedown.

Both players take one card. Each player multiplies her number by the constant factor in the middle. Players *must* verbalize their equations.

> If the players don't verbalize their equations, they don't really have to do any multiplying. They will merely take the cards based on who draws the greater number.

The player with the greater product collects both cards.

Example

It is decided to practice "times 5," so one 5 is placed between the two players. Player 1 draws a 4; Player 2 draws a 7. Players multiply their numbers by 5, and express their equations out loud, "Four times five equals twenty "; "Seven times five equals thirty-five." Player 2 has the greater product so he collects both cards.

If both players have the same product (a tie), each player takes one more card, lays it on top of the first card, and multiplies it by the constant factor. The player with the greater product wins all four cards.

When all the cards in the facedown stack have been used, players count their cards. The player with more cards wins the game.

Questions

- Have you figured out what you already know well and what you need to practice?

- What did you do when you did not know the product of ___ x ___?

- Convince me that ___ x ___ = ___.

Multiplication War

The goal is to draw two factors that when multiplied together result in the greater product.

One-digit multiplication
Variation 1: One-digit multiplication
Variation 2: Multiplying three one-digit factors

Grade 3: CCSS.3.OA.C.7
Grade 4: CCSS.4.NBT.B.5
Grade 5

Two players

Materials

- ten-frame cards 0–5, four of each;
  or standard deck 1–5, four of each

How to play

The cards are shuffled and placed facedown in a stack. Player 1 takes two cards. He multiplies the factors (numbers) and verbalizes the equation; for example, "Four times five equals twenty." Player 2 takes two cards. She multiplies the factors and verbalizes the equation, for instance, "Three times four equals twelve."

The player with the greater product collects all four cards. In case of a tie, each player takes two more cards and multiplies the factors. The player with the greater product collects all eight cards.

When all the facedown cards have been used, the players count their accumulated cards. The player with the most cards is the winner.

> It is very important that players verbalize their equations. If they don't, they may not do the multiplication. They can merely recognize that one player has greater factors and take the four cards based on that fact.

If a player cannot multiply two factors because he does not have the product in instant recall, encourage him to use pencil and paper to figure it out. Don't just give him the answer. One effective way of figuring it out is the tactic used in the "Count the Points" game (page 117).

Questions

- What did you notice about factors and products when you played the game?

- Why was your product greater than or less than the other player's product?

Variation 1: As children gain proficiency at playing this game, it can be modified to include the 6s as factors, then eventually the 7s, and so on.

Variation 2: "Advanced Multiplication War" is played in a similar manner, but the players turn over three cards and multiply the factors (numbers).

Reverse Multiplication Bingo

The goal of this game is to remove all ten counters from the board.

One-digit multiplication

Grade 3: CCSS.3.OA.C.7
Grade 4: CCSS.4.NBT.B.5
Grade 5

Two players

Materials

- ten-frame cards 1–6, four of each; the same if using standard deck
- ten counters for each player, preferably transparent
- "Reverse Multiplication Bingo" game board for each player

1	2	3	4	5	6
7	8	9	10	11	12
13	14	15	16	17	18
19	20	21	22	23	24
25	26	27	28	29	30
31	32	33	34	35	36

How to play

The cards are shuffled and stacked facedown. Players place their counters on any ten products on their boards, making sure the numbers are visible.

Player 1 takes two cards. She multiplies the two factors and verbalizes the equation. If she placed a counter on the product number on her board, she removes the counter from that product. Player 1 puts the two cards in a discard pile.

Example

Player 1 takes a 3 and a 6 and says, "Three times six equals eighteen," and removes the counter from 18 if she had covered that product.

Player 2 draws two cards and proceeds in the same manner.

When the facedown cards in the stack have all been used, the discard pile is shuffled, stacked facedown, and play continues.

The first player to remove all ten counters from their board is the winner.

It will be tempting to point out that there are some numbers on the board that will never be used, but don't do it. Play the game a few more times, and let the children come to that discovery themselves. When they do reach that conclusion, you might ask them why some numbers are never used.

Questions

- What did you discover while playing this game?
- Will you do anything differently the next time?
- What products will you cover in the next game?
- Are there any numbers you won't cover? Why?
- Are there some products that could have been used more than once? Why?

Multiplication Lotto

The goal of the game is to cover four spaces in a vertical, horizontal, or diagonal row.

One-digit multiplication

Grade 3: CCSS.3.OA.C.7
Grade 4: CCSS.4.NBT.B.5
Grade 5

Two players

Materials

- ten-frame cards with 0s and 10s removed, or standard deck with 10s and face cards removed

- die

- counters

- "Multiplicaton Lotto" game board for each player

5	10	15	20	42	25
30	35	40	45	4	8
12	16	20	24	28	32
36	3	48	6	9	12
15	18	21	24	27	2
4	6	8	10	12	14
16	1	2	3	4	5
6	7	54	8	9	18

How to play

The cards are shuffled and stacked facedown.

Player 1 turns over one card for one factor and rolls the die for the second factor. He multiplies the two factors mentally and covers the resulting product on his game board with a counter. Player 2 proceeds in the same manner.

If a resulting product has already been covered with a counter, the player loses a turn.

Play continues until one of the players has covered four spaces in a vertical, horizontal, or diagonal row.

Questions

- What factors are you looking for that might help you cover a product next to one that has already been covered?

- How likely are you to roll a ___?

Multiplication Block It

The goal of this game is to have four counters in a vertical, horizontal, or diagonal row.

One-digit multiplication

Grade 3: CCSS.3.OA.C.7
Grade 4: CCSS.4.NBT.B.5
Grade 5

Two players

Materials

- two paper clips
- different counters for each player
- "Multiplication Block It" game board

more**4U**

1	2	3	4	5	6
7	8	9	10	12	14
15	16	18	20	21	24
25	27	28	30	32	35
36	40	42	45	48	49
54	56	63	64	72	81

Factors   1   2   3   4   5   6   7   8   9

How to play

Player 1 places two paper clips under any two factors below the grid. (The two paper clips can be placed under the same factor.) Player 1 multiplies the two factors and places a counter on the corresponding product on the game board.

From this point on, only one paper clip can be moved.

Player 2 moves one paper clip to a different factor. He multiplies the two factors and places a counter on the resulting product.

Example

Player 1 places one paper clip under 2 and the other under 4 in the factor line. She multiplies 2 x 4 and places a counter on the product, 8, on the game board.

Player 2 leaves one paper clip on the 2 and moves the other paper clip under the 9. He multiplies 2 x 9 and puts his counter on the 18 on the game board.

If a product already has a counter on it, another counter may not be put on top.

Players continue to alternate turns until one player has four counters in a vertical, horizontal, or diagonal row.

This game generates a lot of mental multiplication practice.

When I introduce this game in the classroom, I play it with the whole class. I use a document camera to project the game board, includiing the factor line.

I divide the class in half and the left side of the room (red) plays against the right side of the room (blue). I have found that those round transparent counters, available at many education supply stores, work best. (I'm often asked how I decide which team goes first. There are many possibilities. I always respond, "This is no longer my game. It's yours. You decide. Do what works best for your children.")

One team begins the game by telling me where to put the two paper clips. Almost always, I take the first suggestion I hear. The suggestion maker must give me a full equation, for example. "Put the first paper clip under the four and the second under the six; four times six equals twenty-four." So I put that team's counter on the 24.

It's the other team's turn and they can move only one paper clip. Again, I take the first suggestion I hear.

At some point, the students on both teams begin to disagree about which paper clip should be moved. I give them about a minute to get organized, talk about possible strategies, and decide how they are going to proceed.

Once the game is learned, I pair the students, and they play against each other with paper copies of the game board, counters, and two paper clips.

Questions

- Did you discover any strategies that were helpful while playing this game?

- After looking at the counters already on the board, which products would be helpful because they would get another counter beside one you already have on the board?

- Which factors would you multiply to get this needed product?

- Are there any other factors you could use to get this same product?

- Which products would help you block the other player from getting four in a row?

Salute Multiplication

The goal of this game is to discover the unknown factor.

One-digit multiplication with a missing factor

Grade 3: CCSS.3.OA.A.4
CCSS.3.OA.C.7
Grade 4: CCSS.4.NBT.B.5
Grade 5

Two players

Materials

- ten-frame cards 1–5, four of each;
  the same if using standard deck

How to play

The cards are shuffled and placed facedown in a stack.

Player 1 takes the top card, places it faceup for all to see, and states the factor out loud. Player 2 takes a card and *does not look at it*. Player 2 holds the card on her forehead so that Player 1 can see it, but she can't.

Player 1 *mentally* multiplies the two factors and says out loud, "____ times the factor on your head equals ____." Player 2 listens and figures out what the unknown factor on her head must be and says that factor out loud. If her response is correct, Player 2 keeps both cards. If it isn't correct, Player 2 must find a strategy that will help her figure it out, but she does not keep the cards. They go in a discard pile.

Example

Player 1 turns over a 6 for both players to see. Player 2 puts a 4 on her forehead without looking at it. Player 1 mentally multiplies the two factors and says, "Six times the factor on your head equals twenty-four." Player 2 must figure out what factor times 6 equals 24. She says, "I must have a four on my head because six times four equals twenty-four." Player 2 keeps both cards.

Players reverse roles for the next round. They continue to alternate roles and play until all the cards in the facedown stack have been used. The player with more cards is the winner.

Questions

- You can't figure out what the factor on top of your head is. What can you do to help yourself?

- Which multiplication fact do you already know that might be able to help you?

- Could you draw a picture? Draw horizontal and vertical lines (see the "Count the Points" game on page 117) and count the points? Get some manipulatives?

- Which multiplication facts do you already know? Which ones do you need to practice?

Multiplication Bingo

This game uses multiplication flash cards (available in education supply stores, some bookstores, and online), the products of which are marked on the game board. The goal of the game is to be the first player to fill five spaces in a vertical, horizontal, or diagonal row.

One-digit multiplication

Grade 3: CCSS.3.OA.C.7
Grade 4: CCSS.4.NBT.B.5
Grade 5

Two or more players

Materials

- multiplication flash cards (remove all 0 flash cards except one)
- "Multiplication Bingo" game board for each player

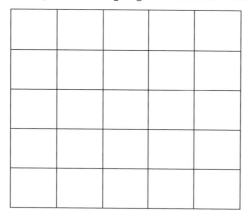

Products: 0, 1, 2, 3, 4, 5, 6, 7, 8, 9, 10, 12, 14, 15, 16, 18, 20, 21, 24, 25, 27, 28, 30, 32, 35, 36, 40, 42, 45, 48, 49, 54, 56, 63, 64, 72, 81

- pencils or crayons

How to play

Players choose twenty-five products from the list under the grid and write one in each square. (It will be helpful to the players to cross off the products as they put each one in a square.)

The teacher or parent shuffles the flash cards and randomly chooses a multiplication fact. He holds up the card, making sure everyone can see it, and verbalizes the fact. Players with that product in their grid color that square (or mark it with an X).

Play continues until a player gets bingo—five in a row, vertically, horizontally, or diagonally.

This game doesn't require fancy flash cards, but the cards do need to be large enough for everyone to see easily.

Before the game starts, make it clear to the children that the product is "top secret" and not to be said out loud. Basically, this is to make sure that everyone is thinking and doing the math.

Questions

- What did you notice when you played this game?
- When you play it a second time, will you make different choices for products to put in the squares? Why?
- Were there any products that could have been used more than once? Why do you think that happened?

Multiplication Unscramble

The goal of the game is to arrange ten multiplication fact cards in a row from smallest product to greatest product.

One-digit multiplication

Grade 3: CCSS.3.OA.C.7
Grade 4: CCSS.4.NBT.B.5
Grade 5

Two players of equal skill

Materials

- multiplication fact cards with no products for numbers 1–9

> If you can't find multiplication fact cards without the answers (products) to purchase, have the children make their own fact cards with 3 x 5-inch index cards (which come in a variety of colors now) and a marker. It's a great math workout for children. Writing the facts is good training for them, and they can practice their mental math to get the products (or if at home, they can verbalize the answers)—but no marking the answers on the cards!

How to play

The fact cards are shuffled and each player receives ten cards facedown. (Players take turns being the dealer.)

The dealer says, "Unscramble," and players turn over all their cards and put them in a row. Players rearrange their cards in order, from smallest to greatest product, by solving the problems on the cards.

Example

Player 1 turns over the following cards:

$6 \times 2, 4 \times 2, 8 \times 3, 5 \times 7, 5 \times 1, 9 \times 7, 2 \times 9, 3 \times 3, 8 \times 6, 5 \times 5$

Player 1 rearranges them in the following order:

$5 \times 1, 4 \times 2, 3 \times 3, 6 \times 2, 2 \times 9, 8 \times 3, 5 \times 5, 5 \times 7, 8 \times 6, 9 \times 7$

When both players have completed this task, they must defend the order of their cards and check each other's multiplication. If the sequence of the cards is correct, the player receives one point. At the end of five rounds, the player with the most points wins.

Questions

- What did you notice about factors and products while playing the game?
- Which products have the most factors?
- Which products have the fewest factors?
- What do you need to practice?

Factor Hunt

The goal of this game is to find the most factors.

One-digit multiplication: finding factors

Grade 3: CCSS.3.OA.C.7
Grade 4: CCSS.4.NBT.B.5
Grade 5

Two players

Materials

- ten-frame cards, or standard deck with face cards removed

- pencils

- "Factor Hunt" recording sheet for each player

Round	Addition Equation				Factors of that sum	Points
1	+	+	+	=		
2	+	+	+	=		
3	+	+	+	=		
4	+	+	+	=		
5	+	+	+	=		
6	+	+	+	=		
						Total points

How to play

The cards are shuffled and placed facedown in a stack. Player 1 turns over four cards. Each player adds these four numbers and writes the equation on the Round 1 line of their recording sheet.

Each player works individually to list as many possible factors of this sum. Players compare answers and get one point for each correct factor.

Example

Player 1 turns over 6, 8, 6, and 4. Both players write these numbers on their recording sheets and find the sum.

6 + 8 + 6 + 4 = 24

Player 1 lists the following factors of 24: 1, 2, 4, 6, 12, and 24.

Player 2 lists the following factors of 24: 1, 2, 3, 4, 6, 8, 12, and 24.

Player 1 gets 6 points; Player 2 gets 8 points.

If a player lists an incorrect factor, he loses one point.

After six rounds, the player with more points wins the game.

Questions

- What did you notice about factors and certain numbers when you played this game?

- How do you know that you found all the factors for that number?

- Did all the sums have factors? Why or why not?

Multiple Multiplication

The goal of the game is to have the greatest product.

Multiple one-digit multiplication
Exponents

Grade 3: CCSS.3.OA.C.7
Grade 4: CCSS.4.NBT.B.5
Grade 5

Two players

Materials

- die
- paper
- pencils
- "Multiple Multiplication" recording sheet for each player

Round	Base Number	Exponent	Equation
1			
2			
3			
4			
5			
6			
7			
8			
9			
10			

How to play

Player 1 rolls the die for the base number. She rolls the die a second time for the exponent. Player 1 records the results on the recording sheet. Player 2 checks Player 1's work for accuracy.

Example

Player 1 rolls the die for a 5. This is the base number. On the second throw of the die, she rolls a 3. This is the exponent. Player 1 multiplies 5 x 5 x 5 = 125.

Player 2 rolls the die and play proceeds in the same manner. The player with the higher product wins the round.

After ten rounds, the player with more winning rounds is the winner of the game.

Questions

- What did you notice while playing the game?

- How did the base numbers and exponents you rolled affect the product?

- What would be the greatest and least product you could have?

Variation: "More Multiple Multiplication" is played in a similar fashion, but ten-frame cards 1 to 9 are used instead of a die. Players take two cards, the first for the base number and the second for the exponent, and then multiply.

Multiplication

Going for the Greatest

The goal of this game is to have the greater product.

Multiplying a two-digit number by a one-digit number

Grade 4: CCSS.4.NBT.B.5

Grade 5

Two players

Materials

- ten-frame cards, or standard deck with face cards removed
- paper
- pencils

How to play

The cards are shuffled and stacked facedown. Player 1 turns over three cards. He selects two and makes a two-digit number; then multiplies it by the third number, writing down his work.

Example

Player 1 turns over 7, 5, and 4, and creates this problem:

$$\begin{array}{r} 54 \\ \times 7 \\ \hline 378 \end{array}$$

Player 2 checks Player 1's work for accuracy. Player 1 puts the three used cards in a discard pile. Player 2 takes three cards and proceeds in the same manner.

The player with the greater product wins a point. Before moving on to the next round, players determine if either of the problems could have been reconfigured to get a greater product. If they find a way to set up either problem for a larger product, they both get an extra point.

Play continues until one player has ten points.

Questions

- What did you notice while playing this game?
- Why did you place your numbers as you did? What was your thinking?
- If you rearranged your numbers, could you make a greater product?
- Did you find any strategies that were helpful in making the greater product?
- Will these same strategies work if you have to make the smallest possible product? Play "Going for the Smallest" and find out.

Variation: "Going for the Smallest" is played the same way, but players set up their problems to make the smallest possible product.

Multiplication Beat the Teacher

This is a whole-class game. The goal is to get a product greater than the teacher's product.

Multiplying a two-digit number by a one-digit number
Variation 1: Multiplying a two-digit number by a one-digit number
Variation 2: Multiplying a two-digit number by a two-digit number

Grade 4: CCSS.4.NBT.B.5
Grade 5

Variation 3: Multiplying a three-digit number by a two-digit number

Grade 4
Grade 5

Multiple players

Materials

- large die
- paper
- pencils

How to play

The game is played for a predetermined amount of time. The teacher draws a large grid on the board (see below) for all to see. The children draw the same grid on their papers. (Grids may also be downloaded and printed, if desired.) The teacher also has a paper grid for himself.

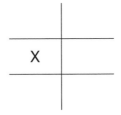

The teacher instructs the class that numbers can only be put into the three empty spaces in the top two rows; no number can be put in the space with the "x" or in the bottom two spaces.

The teacher will roll the die a total of three times, calling out the number with each roll of the die. The children must immediately put the number into any one of the top three spaces on the grid. **Once written, the number cannot be moved to a different space.** The teacher does the same on his paper grid but does not reveal his placement of the number to the class.

I often check to make sure the children are immediately writing the number in a space. Also, if necessary, make them play the game with a pen or crayon so they are not tempted to move the number to a different space later in the game.

When the three spaces are filled, everyone multiplies the two-digit number by the one-digit number, and places the product in the bottom two spaces. Players trade papers and check each other's multiplication, initialing it if it is correct.

The teacher reveals his paper grid and fills the spaces of the grid on the board with his numbers and product. Students who have a product that is greater than the teacher's product "beat the teacher" and get two points. Students with a product equal to the teacher's get one point.

At the end of the game session, the players with the most points are the winners.

Questions

Here are some questions to ask after the first round of play:

- What strategies have you discovered that will help you make a greater product?
- Now that you know how the game is played, what will you do differently in the next round?
- What did _____(name of child) do differently that allowed her to have a greater product than the teacher?
- What have you learned about the placing of factors to get the greatest product?
- Will you use the same strategies if you have to make a product that is less than the teacher's?
- How likely was it that a _____that you needed would be rolled?

Variation 1: The game is played in the same way, but the goal is to create a product that is less than the teacher's to win two points.

Variation 2: "Double-Digit Multiplication Beat the Teacher" is played in a similar manner, but the die is rolled four times, and players make two two-digit numbers to multiply for the greatest product.

Variation 3: "Multidigit Multipilication Beat the Teacher" is played in a similar manner, but the die is rolled five times, and players make one three-digit number to multiply by a two-digit number. They will need a nine-space grid for this game.

Strategy Multiplication

Here's a way to "beat the teacher" without the teacher! The object of this game is to make the greatest product possible.

Multiplying a two-digit number by a one-digit number
Variation 1: Multiplying a two-digit number by a one-digit number
Variation 2: Multiplying a two-digit number by a two-digit number
Variation 3: Multiplying a three-digit number by a two-digit number

Grade 4: CCSS.4.NBT.B.5
Grade 5

Two or more players

Materials

- ten-frame cards, 10s removed, or standard deck with 10s and face cards removed

- paper

- pencils

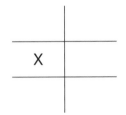

How to play

The game is played for a predetermined amount of time. The players draw a multiplication grid on a piece of paper. (Grids may also be downloaded and printed, if desired.) They are reminded that numbers can only be put into the three empty spaces in the top two rows; no number can be put in the space with the "x" or in the bottom two spaces.

The cards are shuffled and stacked facedown. Player 1 draws a card that is placed faceup for both players to see.

Players must immediately put the number into any one of the top three spaces on their grid. **Once written, the number cannot be moved to a different space**.

Player 2 draws a card that is placed faceup for both players to see. Again, each player selects a space on their grid and writes the number of this card in it.

Player 1 draws the third and final card and each player puts the number in the remaining open space. (If more than two children are playing, players rotate turns drawing a card.)

When the three spaces are filled, the players multiply the two-digit number by the one-digit number, and place the product in the bottom two spaces. Players trade papers and check each other's multiplication, initialing it if it is correct.

The player with the greatest product scores one point. At the end of the game session, the player with the most points is the winner.

Questions

- What strategies have you discovered that will help you make a greater product?

- Now that you know how the game is played, what will you do differently in the next round?

- What have you discovered about factors and where they should be placed?

- What did _____(name of child) do differently that allowed her to have a greater product than you?

- Will you use the same strategies if you have to make the smallest product possible?

- How likely were you to draw the _____that you needed?

Variation 1: The game is played in the same way, but the goal is to create a product that is less than any other player's to win a point.

Variation 2: "Two-Digit Strategy Multiplication" is played in a similar manner, but four cards are drawn, and players make two two-digit numbers to multiply for the greatest product.

Variation 3: "Multidigit Strategy Multiplication" is played in a similar manner, but five cards are drawn, and players make one three-digit number to multiply by a two-digit number. They will need a nine-space grid for this game.

Target—300

The goal of this game is to be as close to 300 as possible after six rolls of the die. Players must play six rounds; even if they are very close to 300, they cannot stop sooner. This is not an "exact" game so the sum of the products can be more than 300.

Multiplying one-digit numbers by multiples of 10

Grade 3: CCSS.3.NBT.A.3
Grade 4: CCSS.4.NBT.B.5
Grade 5: CCSS.5.NBT.A.2

Two or more players

Materials

- die

- pencil

- "Target—300" recording sheet for each player

Roll	Equation (Multiply by 10, 20, 30, 40, or 50.)
1	
2	
3	
4	
5	
6	
	Sum of products_____
	I was _____ from 300.

How to play

Player 1 rolls the die. Each player decides whether to multiply the number on the die by 10, 20, 30, 40, or 50, knowing that there will be six rolls of the die to get as close to 300 as possible. Each player writes his multiplication equation on his recording sheet.

Example

Player 1 rolls a 2 and decides to multiply it by 30, and writes it on his recording sheet as—

Roll	Equation (Multiply by 10, 20, 30, 40, or 50.)
1	2 x 30 = 60

Players exchange sheets and check each other's multiplication for accuracy.

Player 2 rolls the die and players proceed in the same manner.

Players continue to take turns rolling the die until six rounds have been played. The player whose product sum is closest to 300 is the winner.

Questions

- What did you notice after playing this game once?
- Did you discover any helpful strategies?
- What will you do differently the next time you play this game?
- How did you figure out how close your product sum was to 300?

Move-It-Around Multiplication

The object of the game is to make the greatest possible product.

Multiplying a two-digit number by a one-digit number
Variation: Multiplying a two-digit number by a two-digit number

Grade 4: CCSS.4.NBT.B.5
Grade 5

Two or more players

Materials

- ten-frame cards with 10s removed, or standard deck
  with 10s and face cards removed

- paper

- pencils

How to play

The cards are shuffled and stacked facedown. Player 1 takes three cards and lays them out for all the players to see. Players use these three numbers to create a two-digit number to multiply by a one-digit number to get the greatest possible product.

Players write their multiplication problem down and compare products. The player with the greatest product scores one point. If players have the same winning product (a tie), they both score one point.

Players continue to play until one player accumulates ten points.

Questions

- Did you discover a strategy that helped you get the greatest product?

- Did that strategy work no matter which numbers were used?

Variation: "More Move-It-Around Multiplication" is played in the same way, but four cards are drawn to create two two-digit numbers to multiply for the greatest possible product.

The Games

Division

Introduction

Division Glossary 150

Dividing a One- or Two-Digit Dividend by a One-Digit Divisor

Leftovers 151

The Constant Quotient 153

Division Bingo 154

Division Memory Concentration 156

Division Beat the Teacher 158

Division Challenge 160

What Remains? 162

Dividing a Three- or Four-Digit Dividend by a One-Digit Divisor

Three-Car Garage Beat the Teacher 159

Three-Digit Dividend Challenge 161

Four-Digit Dividend Challenge 161

Estimate and Divide 163

Dividing a Three- or Four-Digit Dividend by a Two-Digit Divisor

Two-Digit Divisor Beat the Teacher 159

Two-Digit Divisor Challenge 161

Super Two-Digit Divisor Challenge 161

Introduction

The Common Core State Standards for Mathematics first mentions the operation of division in the standards for the third grade (NGA and CCSSO 2010, p. 23, 3.OA).

Division can be challenging for children. They come to school understanding how to *share*, yet when it's called *division*, they somehow lose that skill. Division is sharing—sharing equally into groups. For example, 12 ÷ 4 is really just breaking 12 apart into 4 equal groups.

In order to learn division, it's helpful if children have a good understanding of multiplication. Children don't need to be perfect, but they should know the majority of the facts or have a reasonably quick strategy to figure out the answer.

One of the keys to teaching division so that most students will understand and retain the information is to make it fun. Worksheets rarely, if ever, do that.

The following games not only make division fun but also require children to use critical thinking skills.

Division Glossary

When playing math games, it is important that the children become familiar with the correct math terminology for certain facts and concepts. In this section there are seven words that should be introduced and consistently used; their definitions are below.

Division is the sharing of or grouping of a number into equal parts.

Dividend is the number being divided.

Divisor is a number that will divide the dividend.

Quotient is the result of a division; the answer to a division problem.

Factor (divisor) is a number that divides a larger number exactly, for example, 2 and 10 are factors of 20.

$$\underset{\text{dividend}}{20} \quad \div \quad \underset{\text{divisor}}{2} \quad = \quad \underset{\text{quotient}}{10}$$

Equal is having the same amount or identical value.

Equation, sometimes called a number sentence, is a mathematical statement containing an equals sign (=) that shows that two expressions are equal.

Leftovers

The goal of this game is to have the fewer "leftovers."

Division

Grade 3: CCSS.3.OA.C.7
Grade 4: CCSS.4.NBT.B.6
Grade 5

Two players

Materials

- die
- paper
- pencils

How to play

Each player picks a number between 10 and 30, writes that number on her paper, and then proceeds to draw that many Xs on the paper.

Example

Player 1 picks the number 12 and draws twelve Xs on his paper.

Player 2 picks the number 28 and draws twenty-eight Xs on her paper.

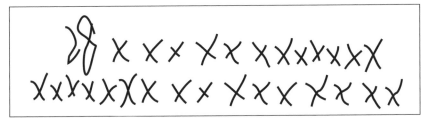

Player 1 rolls the die. Each player draws circles around the Xs in groups of the rolled number .

Example

Player 1 rolls a 4. Players circle their Xs in groups of 4.

Those Xs outside the circles are the "leftovers." The player with fewer leftovers is the winner.

Questions

- What did you discover while playing this game?

- What strategies were helpful in deciding which number between 10 and 30 to use?

<u>Variation:</u> The game is played in the same way, but two dice are rolled and added together to get the divisor. Be sure to increase the number of Xs to be drawn to at least 12 to 36.

The Constant Quotient

The goal of the game is to write down as many division facts as possible using a particular quotient in one minute. The game requires an adult or third player to act as a timekeeper.

Division

Grade 3: CCSS.3.OA.C.7
Grade 4: CCSS.4.NBT.B.6
Grade 5

Two or more players

One timekeeper

Materials

- ten-frame cards 2–10, two of each; the same if using standard deck

mor4U

- paper

- pencils

How to play

The cards are shuffled and placed facedown in a stack. The timekeeper turns over the top card, displays it to the players, and says, "Go!" Players have one minute to write as many division facts as they can that have that number as the quotient.

Example

The timekeeper turns over a 2, shows it to the players, and says, "Go!"

Player 1 writes down $4 \div 2 = 2$, $6 \div 3 = 2$, $8 \div 4 = 2$, $12 \div 6 = 2$, and so on.

At the end of one minute, the timekeeper says, "Stop!" Players check each other's work and are awarded one point for each correct division fact that has the selected number as the quotient.

The timekeeper turns over another card for a new quotient, and the second round begins. After ten rounds, the player with the most points is the winner.

Questions

- What did you discover about yourself while playing this game?

- What do you need to practice?

- Were there any facts that were harder than others?

- How did you help yourself while playing this game?

Division Bingo

This game provides practice with any division facts you choose. The goal of the game is to cross off three quotients in a vertical, horizontal, or diagonal row.

Division

Grade 3: CCSS.3.OA.C.7
Grade 4: CCSS.4.NBT.B.6
Grade 5

Two players

Materials

- paper

- pencils

- division fact cards with no quotients (see sample below) for numbers 1–9

- "Division Bingo" bingo board for each player

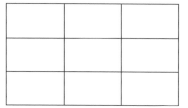

> If you can't find division fact cards without the answers (quotients) to purchase, have the children make their own fact cards with 3 x 5-inch index cards (which come in a variety of colors now) and a marker. It's a great math workout for children. Writing the facts is good training for them, and they can practice their mental math to get the quotients (or if at home, they can verbalize the answers)—but no marking the answers on the cards!

Division fact cards for 7

7 ÷ 7	14 ÷ 7	21 ÷ 7	28 ÷ 7	35 ÷ 7
42 ÷ 7	49 ÷ 7	56 ÷ 7	63 ÷ 7	70 ÷ 7

How to play

In each space on the game board, players write nine numbers (quotients) from 1 to 10 (one number will be left out). Players may arrange the numbers in any order they wish. The division fact cards are shuffled and stacked facedown.

> Children need a solid foundation on which to build their math skills. Until children have the basic division facts in long-term memory (quotients from 1 to 10), it can be very frustrating and unproductive for them—and you—to move on to harder ones.

Player 1 turns over the top fact card and solves the problem out loud; for example, "Twenty-one divided by seven equals three." If the quotient matches a number on Player 1's bingo board, he marks an X through the number. The card is placed in a discard pile.

Player 2 turns over a fact card and proceeds in the same manner.

When all the cards in the facedown stack have been used, the discard pile is shuffled and stacked, and play continues.

The first player to cross out three quotients in a vertical, horizontal, or diagonal row wins the game.

For each game, players use a new bingo board, placing the quotients in different spaces.

Questions

- When you play this game again, will you place your quotients differently? Why or why not?
- What quotient did you leave off your grid? Will you leave the same quotient off the next round?
- Did you find a strategy for picking and placing quotients in your grid?
- Will your strategy work if using different fact cards?
- What do you need to practice?

Division

Division Memory Concentration

This game provides practice with any division facts you choose. The goal of this game is to find a quotient card that equals a division fact card.

Division

Grade 3: CCSS.3OA.C.7
Grade 4: CCSS.4.NBT.B.6
Grade 5

Two players

Materials

- division fact cards with no quotients (see sample below)
- "Division Memory Concentration" division quotient cards

2	3	4
5	6	7
8	9	10

> If you can't find division fact cards without the answers (quotients) to purchase, have the children make their own fact cards with 3 x 5-inch index cards (which come in a variety of colors now) and a marker. It's a great math workout for children. As they write the facts, they can practice their mental math to get the quotients (or if at home, they can verbalize the answers)—but no marking the answers on the cards!

Division fact cards for 9

18 ÷ 9	27 ÷ 9	36 ÷ 9
45 ÷ 9	54 ÷ 9	63 ÷ 9
72 ÷ 9	81 ÷ 9	90 ÷ 9

Pregame practice

The practice session with the cards *faceup* allows the children to see what they are expected to do mathematically.

The fact cards are shuffled and arranged faceup in three rows with three cards in each row.

The quotient cards are shuffled and placed faceup in three rows with three cards in each row next to the fact cards. Player 1 selects a fact card and looks for the quotient card that matches. Player 1 must verbalize the complete equation to her partner. Player 1 takes both cards after correctly giving the equation.

Example

Player 1 selects 36 ÷ 9 and says, "Thirty-six divided by nine equals four." Player 1 takes both the fact and quotient cards.

Player 2 selects a fact card and proceeds in the same manner. Players take turns finding all the matches.

How to play

Each set of cards is shuffled and arranged facedown in three rows with three cards in each row, one set next to the other.

Player 1 turns over a fact card and verbalizes the fact and states the quotient card he is looking for.

Example

Player 1 turns over a fact card, keeping it in place, and says, "Eighteen divided by nine. I am looking for the quotient card two because eighteen divided by nine equals two."

Player 1 turns over a quotient card, keeping it in place. If the fact card and quotient card are equal, Player 1 takes both cards. If they are not equal, Player 1 turns both cards back over, and it is Player 2's turn.

Players alternate turns. When all the cards have been matched, players count their cards. The player with more cards wins the game.

Questions

- When players turn over the fact card, ask them what quotient they are looking for. If they aren't sure, ask them what they can do to help themselves figure it out. Draw a picture? Use counters?
- What facts do you know for sure?
- Which ones do you need to practice?

Division Beat the Teacher

This is a whole-class or whole-group game. The goal of this game is to get a quotient that is less than the teacher's quotient.

Dividing a two-digit number by a one-digit number
Variation 1: Dividing a two-digit number by a one-digit number

Grade 3: CCSS.3.OA.C.7
Grade 4: CCSS.4.NBT.B.6

Variation 2: Dividing a three-digit number by a one-digit number
Variation 3: Dividing a three-digit number by a two-digit number

Grade 4: CCSS.4.NBT.B.6
Grade 5

Multiple players

Materials

- large die
- paper
- pencils

How to play

The game is played for a predetermined amount of time. The teacher draws a large "garage" on the board with one line to the left for the divisor and two lines inside the garage for a two-digit dividend. The children draw the same garage on their papers. The teacher also has a paper copy for his personal use.

The teacher instructs the class that numbers can be put only into the two spaces in the garage or the space to the left of the garage.

The teacher rolls the die a total of three times, calling out the number with each roll of the die. The children must immediately put the number into any one of the three spaces, but **once written, the number cannot be moved to a different space.** The teacher does the same on his paper but does not reveal his placement of the number to the class.

> I often check to make sure the children are immediately writing their number in a space. Also, if necessary, make them play the game with a pen or crayon so they are not tempted to move the number to a different space later in the game.

When the three spaces are filled, everyone divides the two-digit number by the one-digit number and places the quotient on the "roof" of the division garage. Players trade papers and check each other's division, initialing it if it is correct.

The teacher reveals his paper and fills the spaces of the garage on the board with his numbers and his quotient. Students who have a quotient that is less than the teacher's quotient "beat the teacher" and get two points. Students who have a quotient equal to the teacher's quotient get one point.

At the end of the game session, the players with the most points are the winners.

Questions

Here are some questions to ask after the first round of play:

- What strategies have you discovered that will help you to make a smaller quotient?

- Now that you know how the game is played, what will you do differently the next round?

- What did _____(name of child) do differently that allowed her to have a smaller quotient than the teacher's?

- What have you learned about the placing of numbers to get the smallest quotient?

- Will you use the same strategies if you have to make a quotient greater than the teacher's?

- How likely was it that a _____ that you needed would be rolled?

Variation 1: The game is played in the same way, but the goal is to create a quotient that is greater than the teacher's to win two points.

Variation 2: "Three-Car Garage Beat the Teacher" is played in a similar manner, but the die is rolled four times, and players make a three-digit number to be divided by a one-digit number.

Variation 3: "Two-Digit Divisor Beat the Teacher" is played in a similar manner, but the die is rolled five times, and players make a three-digit number to be divided by a two-digit divisor.

Division Challenge

No teacher is needed to play this version of "Beat the Teacher." The object of this game is to make the smallest quotient possible.

Dividing a two-digit number by a one-digit number
Variation 1: Dividing a two-digit number by a one-digit number

Grade 3: CCSS.3.OA.C.7
Grade 4: CCSS.4.NBT.B.6

Variations 2–5: Greater dividends and divisors

Grade 5

Two or more players

Materials

- ten-frame cards with 10s removed, or
  standard deck with 10s and face cards removed

- paper

- pencils

How to play

The cards are shuffled and stacked facedown. Players draw the division "garage" on their papers with one line to the left for the divisor and two lines inside the garage for a two-digit dividend. Players are reminded that numbers can only be put into the two spaces in the garage or the space to the left of the garage.

$$\underline{} \,) \, \overline{\underline{} \ \underline{}}$$

Player 1 draws a card that is placed faceup for the other players to see. Each player must immediately put the number into any one of the three spaces. **Once written, the number cannot be moved to a different space.**

Player 2 draws a card that is placed faceup for the players to see. Again, each player selects a space and writes the number of this card in it.

Player 1 draws the third and final card and each player puts the number in the remaining open space. (If more than two children are playing, players rotate turns drawing a card.)

When the three spaces are filled, players divide their two-digit number by the one-digit number and place the quotient on the "roof" of the division garage. Players trade papers and check each other's division, initialing it if it is correct.

The player with the smallest quotient is the winner of that round and scores a point. The winner of the game is the player with the most points after ten rounds.

Questions

- What will you do differently in the next round?

- Have you discovered a strategy that helps you get the smallest quotient?

- Will that same strategy work if you have to make the greatest quotient?

- What did the other player do differently that helped him make the smallest quotient? Why did this make a difference?

Variation 1: The game is played in the same way, but the goal is to create the greatest quotient to score a point.

Variation 2: "Three-Digit Dividend Challenge" is played in a similar manner, but four cards are drawn, and players make a three-digit dividend to be divided by a one-digit divisor.

Variation 3: "Four-Digit Dividend Challenge" is played in a similar manner, but five cards are drawn, and players make a four-digit dividend to be divided by a one-digit divisor.

Variation 4: "Two-Digit Divisor Challenge" is played in a similar manner, but five cards are drawn, and players make a three-digit dividend to be divided by a two-digit divisor.

Variation 5: "Super Two-Digit Divisor Challenge" is played in a similar manner, but six cards are drawn, and players make one four-digit dividend to be divided by a two-digit divisor.

Division

What Remains?

The goal of this game is to have the smallest possible remainder.

Dividing a two-digit number by a one-digit number

Grade 3: CCSS.3.OA.C.7
Grade 4: CCSS.4.NBT.B.6
Grade 5

Two players

Materials

- ten-frame cards with 0s and 10s removed, or standard deck with 10s and face cards removed
- paper
- pencils

mor**4U**

How to play

The game is played for a predetermined amount of time. The cards are shuffled and stacked facedown.

Player 1 takes three cards; Player 2 does the same. Both players then arrange their cards into a division problem resulting in the smallest possible remainder.

Example

Player 1 draws 4, 7, and a 3. She can make—

74 ÷ 3 = 24 2R
47 ÷ 3 = 15 2R
37 ÷ 4 = 9 1R
73 ÷ 4 = 18 1R
43 ÷ 7 = 6 1R
34 ÷ 7 = 4 6R

Player 1 would choose one of the division problems with a remainder of 1.

Players check each other's work, and the player with the lesser remainder scores one point. Used cards are placed in a discard pile.

At the end of the game session, the winner is the player with more points.

Questions

- How did you decide which numbers to use in which positions?
- What strategy was helpful in allowing you to have the smallest remainder?
- Will that strategy work in every situation?

Estimate and Divide

The game's goal is to make an estimate that is closest to the actual average of three numbers.

Division
Averaging
Grade 3: CCSS.3.OA.C.7
Grade 4: CCSS.4.NBT.B.6
Grade 5

Two players

Materials

- ten-frame cards with 0s and 10s removed, or standard deck with 10s and face cards removed

- paper

- pencils

How to play

The cards are shuffled and stacked facedown. Player 1 takes the top three cards and makes a three-digit number. Both players record this three-digit number on paper. The cards are put in a discard pile.

Player 2 takes the next three cards in the stack and makes a three-digit number. Both players record this three-digit number. The three cards are put in the discard pile.

Player 1 again takes the top three cards from the stack and makes a three-digit number. Both players record this three-digit number. The three cards are put in the discard pile.

Each player looks at the three three-digit numbers and mentally estimates their average. Players write their estimates on the top of their papers and circle it.

Both players then calculate the sum of the three numbers and divide by 3. Players check each other's work for accuracy and initial if correct. The player whose estimate is closest to the actual average is the winner of that round and receives one point.

After ten rounds of play, the player with more points is the winner.

> When children begin to play this game, it's unlikely that they will have had much experience making estimates, and their estimates won't be very "smart." This game should be played often. It is a great way to give them that experience. After all, as an adult, we make estimates every day of our lives!

Questions

- How did you decide on your estimate?
- Did it work or will you try another strategy?
- Did your estimate get closer to the actual average the more rounds you played?

Multiple Operations

Introduction

Operation Cards 166

Addition and Subtraction

Are They Equal? 167

Balancing Both Sides—Addition and Subtraction 169

Benchmark Numbers 171

Addition and Multiplication

Additional Multiplying 173

Addition, Subtraction, Multiplication, and Division

The Number Ladder Game 175

Take Them Off the Board 177

Operation Bingo 179

Next-Door Neighbors 181

Six = The Seventh 183

Target—24 185

The Elevator Game 187

The Add-to-It Equation Game 189

Multiple Operations Target 191

The Challenge 193

The Operation Game 195

Introduction

In real-life activities, we do various combinations of adding, subtracting, multiplying, and dividing frequently. When we buy a car, follow a recipe, or decorate our home, we're using several different operations of mathematics almost simultaneously. But when we do mathematics in school, oftentimes we do just one operation and then move on to another. When doing so, there's no indication that all of these operations are interrelated or that they will be used together as we live our lives. The following games address that oversight by including more than one operation.

Be aware that in many of the following games, children will be building equations. Make certain that the equations are correct and not just run-ons! For example—

Correct equation: $2 + 3 + 5 = 4 + 6$
Incorrect equation: $2 + 3 = 5 + 2 = 7$

Operation Cards

While playing some of these games, operation cards are needed. A sample is shown below. The templates for the operations cards are available for downloading on the NCTM More4U web page (nctm.org/more4u).

- Print the cards on card stock.

- Laminate them if possible. Many education supply stores have laminating machines. This really helps with longevity.

- Cut them apart and begin to play.

+	−	×	÷
+	−	×	÷
+	−	×	÷
+	−	×	÷
=	=	=	=
(	)	(	)

So let's get real and play some games where players are required to use various combinations of all the operations.

Are They Equal?

The goal of this game is to find an addition fact and a subtraction fact whose sum and difference are equal (have the same value).

Addition and subtraction

Grade 3: CCSS.3.NBT.A.2
Grade 4
Grade 5

Two players

Materials

- addition fact cards

4 + 3	5 + 1	2 + 3
3 + 1	1 + 2	2 + 0
1 + 1	2 + 5	4 + 2
0 + 5	2 + 2	2 + 1
3 + 3	1 + 3	0 + 3

- subtraction fact cards

10 – 3	11 – 5	7 – 3
9 – 4	8 – 4	7 – 1
9 – 6	12 – 10	8 – 5
9 – 7	11 – 4	5 – 2
8 – 2	10 – 5	10 – 6

Pregame practice

The practice session with the cards *faceup* allows the children to visually see what they are expected to do mathematically.

All the addition cards are turned faceup in a grid of three rows with five cards in each row. To one side of the addition cards, all the subtraction cards are turned faceup in a grid of three rows with five cards in each row.

Players take turns finding one addition fact and matching it to one subtraction fact whose difference equals the sum of the addition card. When a player has selected an addition card, she verbalizes the equation, including the sum, and then states the corresponding difference of the subtraction card she is looking for. Once she finds a subtraction card with the matching difference, Player 1 takes both cards and verbalizes the entire equation.

Example

Player 1 picks up the addition card 4 + 3 and says, "Four plus three equals seven. I am looking for a subtraction card whose difference equals seven." She finds 10 − 3 and says to the other player, "Ten minus three equals seven. Because both equations equal seven, I can say four plus three equals ten minus three" (4 + 3 = 10 − 3).

Player 2 selects an addition card and play proceeds in the same manner, with players alternating turns, until all the cards are matched.

How to play

Turn all the addition cards *facedown* in a grid of three rows with five cards in each row. To one side of the addition cards, turn all the subtraction cards *facedown* in a grid of three rows with five cards in each row.

Player 1 turns over one addition card, keeping it in place, reads it aloud with its sum to the other player, and states the difference of the subtraction card he is looking for. Player 1 turns over one subtraction card, keeping it in place.

If Player 1 finds a subtraction fact whose difference has the same value as the sum of his addition fact, he keeps both cards and verbalizes the complete equation for Player 2. If the sum and difference do not have the same value, both cards are turned back over, and it is the Player 2's turn.

Players alternate turns until all the cards are matched. The player with more cards wins the game.

Questions

- What difference are you looking for that has the same value as that sum?

- If you're looking for that difference, what combinations might you find?

Balancing Both Sides—Addition and Subtraction

The object of the game is to balance both sides of the equation by arranging the cards into one addition problem and one subtraction problem with an equal sum and difference.

Addition and subtraction

Grade 3: CCSS.3.NBT.A.2
Grade 4
Grade 5

Two players

Materials

- ten-frame cards, or standard deck with face cards removed
- "Balancing Both Sides" game board for each player

___ + ___ = ___ − ___

How to play

The cards are shuffled and dealt. (Players take turns being the dealer.) Each player gets eight cards. The remaining cards are stacked facedown between the two players.

Player 1 chooses four cards from her hand to place on the game board to make a balanced equation. **Players must use four cards.** A player earns one point for balancing the equation.

Example

Player 1's eight cards are 9, 7, 1, 5, 4, 3, 1, and 8. She could place 7 + 1 on one side of the equals (=) sign and 9 − 1 on the other, 7 + 1 = 9 − 1.

Both facts equal 8, so both sides of the equation have the same value, and the game board is balanced.

Player 2 must check the addition and subtraction facts to make sure that Player 1 has balanced her game board. If she has done so, Player 1 gets one point. Her eight cards are placed at the bottom of the facedown stack.

Player 2 chooses four cards from his hand of eight to place on the board, and play continues in the same manner, with his cards also placed at the bottom of the facedown stack.

After each round of play, the cards are shuffled and each player gets eight new cards for the next round. Play continues in the same manner, with players always checking each other's board to make sure that the equation is balanced.

If the eight cards cannot be arranged in a balanced equation, the player loses a turn, placing his cards at the bottom of the facedown stack.

The game ends when one player reaches ten points.

Questions

- What does the left side of the equation equal? Right side? Are they balanced? Do they have the same value?

- Could this have been set up using different numbers and still be balanced?

- Does it matter which side of the equal sign is the addition side and which side is the subtraction side?

Benchmark Numbers

The goal of the game is to find two "Benchmark Numbers" cards whose sums or differences have the same value. The cards may be two addition cards, two subtraction cards, or one addition card and one subtraction card.

Addition and subtraction

Grade 3: CCSS.3.NBT.A.2
Grade 4
Grade 5

Two players

Materials

- "Benchmark Numbers" cards

75 + 25	50 + 50	50 + 25	100 – 25
60 + 40	10 + 90	25 + 25	85 – 10
51 + 49	95 + 5	100 – 50	20 + 5
75 – 25	51 – 1	65 + 10	30 + 20
1 + 24	10 + 15	45 + 5	26 – 1
35 –1 0	50 – 25	74 + 1	76 – 1

Pregame

The practice session with the cards *faceup* allows the children to visually see what they are expected to do mathematically.

The cards are shuffled and placed faceup in a grid of six rows with four cards in each row. Player 1 picks up one card and says the fact out loud to the other player. He then finds another card that equals the sum or difference of the first and verbalizes that fact, too. If Player 1 has chosen correctly, he keeps the two cards because they both have the same value.

Example

Player 1 selects 50 + 25 and says, "Fifty plus twenty-five equals seventy-five. I am looking for another card that equals seventy-five." He finds a second card that equals 75 and says that fact out loud, "One hundred minus twenty-five equals seventy-five."

Player 2 selects a card and play proceeds in the same manner. Players alternate turns until all the cards are matched.

How to play

The cards are shuffled and placed facedown in a grid of six rows with four cards in each row.

Player 1 turns over one card, keeping it in place, and says the fact and what he is looking for out loud to the other player.

Example

Player 1 turns over the 1 + 24 card. He says to Player 2, "One plus twenty-four equals twenty-five. I am looking for another card that equals twenty-five."

Player 1 turns over a second card, keeping it in place. If it has the same value as the first card, he keeps both cards. If it doesn't, he turns both cards back over in place.

Player 2 proceeds in the same manner.

Players alternate turns until all the cards are matched. The player with more cards wins the game.

Questions

- What did you discover while playing this game?
- What was easy? What was more difficult?

Additional Multiplying

This game uses multiplication to create two products. The goal of the game is to add the two products and have the greater sum.

One-digit multiplication

Grade 3: CCSS.3.OA.C.7
Grade 4: CCSS.4.NBT.B.5
Grade 5

Two-digit addition

Grade 3: CCSS.3.NBT.A.2
Grade 4: CCSS.4.NBT.B.4
Grade 5

Two players

Materials

- ten-frame cards, or standard deck with face cards removed
- pencils
- "Additional Multiplying" recording sheet for each player

Round 1	Round 2	Round 3
___ x ___ = ___ ___ x ___ = ___ Sum ___	___ x ___ = ___ ___ x ___ = ___ Sum ___	___ x ___ = ___ ___ x ___ = ___ Sum___
Round 4	Round 5	Round 6
___ x ___ = ___ ___ x ___ = ___ Sum ___	___ x ___ = ___ ___ x ___ = ___ Sum ___	___ x ___ = ___ ___ x ___ = ___ Sum ___
Round 7	Round 8	Grand Total Add the sums for each round.
___ x ___ = ___ ___ x ___ = ___ Sum ___	___ x ___ = ___ ___ x ___ = ___ Sum___	

How to play

The cards are shuffled and stacked facedown. Player 1 turns over two cards to use as factors. He multiplies the numbers and records this equation on the first line of round 1 on his recording sheet. He puts the used cards in a discard pile.

Player 2 takes two cards and proceeds in the same manner.

Player 1 turns over two more cards, multiplies the factors, and puts this equation on the second line of Round 1 on his recording sheet. He then finds the sum of the two products.

Example

Round 1
$4 \times 5 = 20$
$3 \times 6 = 18$
Sum   38

Player 2 turns over two more cards and proceeds in the same manner.

After eight rounds of play, each player adds the sums of all eight rounds for a grand total. The player with the greater total sum wins the game.

Questions

- Why did you end up with a sum less than (or greater than) the other player?
- Are there any strategies to be used in this game?

The Number Ladder Game

The goal of this game is to use addition, subtraction, multiplication, and division to create simple equations that correlate to the rungs of the ladder.

Addition, subtraction, multiplication, and division

Grade 3
Grade 4
Grade 5

Two players

Materials

- ten-frame cards, or standard deck with face cards removed

- pencils

- "The Number Ladder Game" recording sheet for each player

```
10 = [        ]
 9 = [        ]
 8 = [        ]
 7 = [        ]
 6 = [        ]
 5 = [        ]
 4 = [        ]
 3 = [        ]
 2 = [        ]
 1 = [        ]
```

How to play

The cards are shuffled and each player is dealt ten cards. (Players take turns being the dealer.) The remaining cards are put aside; they will not be needed. Players use their ten cards throughout the game.

Player 1 searches his ten cards for a way to fill in the first rung of his ladder with an equation that equals 1 by adding, subtracting, multiplying, or dividing the numbers in his ten cards. He writes that equation on his first rung.

Player 2 checks Player 1's equation for accuracy, and then searches her ten cards for a way to do the same. Player 1 checks to make sure Player 2's equation is correct.

Each card may be used only once in a single equation, but all ten cards may be used again for the next equation.

Players alternate turns, working their way up the ladder until they can no longer make an equation to equal the next rung's number. The highest rung reached is the player's score.

10 =	4 + 6
9 =	4 x 2 + 1
8 =	4 x 2
7 =	3 + 4
6 =	2 x 3
5 =	3 + 2
4 =	2 x 2
3 =	9 ÷ 3
2 =	2 + 0
1 =	3 – 2

Questions

- What was the easiest thing about playing this game? The hardest?

- Look at your ten cards. Are there any other ways you could have equaled ____?

- I see you made ____ by using addition. Is there another way you could have made ____ using subtraction? Multiplication? Division?

Variation: Play the game the same way but create a longer ladder by adding larger numbers on top or start the ladder with a higher number.

Take Them Off the Board

This game provides practice and insights into the relationship of numbers and how the same numbers can produce different results with different operations (addition, subtraction, multiplication, and division). The goal of the game is to eliminate as many numbers in the number line as possible.

Addition, subtraction, multiplication, and division

Grade 3
Grade 4
Grade 5

Two players

Materials

- Two dice

- pencils

- Set of 0–12 cards for each player

0	1	2
3	4	5
6	7	8
9	10	11
12		

- "Take Them Off the Board" recording sheet for each player

Take Them Off the Board				
Turn	Addition	Subtraction	Multiplication	Division
1				
2				
3				
4				
5				
6				
7				
8				
9				
10				

How to play

Players arrange their cards faceup in a line of numbers from left to right.

Player 1 rolls the dice. The numbers on the dice are added, subtracted, multiplied, and divided. For example, the results of a throw of a 6 and a 2 can be 8 (6 + 2 = 8), 4 (6 − 2 = 4), 12 (6 x 2 = 12), or 3 (6 ÷ 2 = 3). Player 1 records all possible equations for that turn on his recording sheet. If the numbers on the dice cannot be divided equally, for example, 5 and 3, there will be no equation listed under Division.

Player 1 selects one of his equations, and highlights (or circles) that equation on his recording sheet. He tells the other player what he is doing, and takes that number out of the number line.

Example

Take Them Off the Board				
Turn	Addition	Subtraction	Multiplication	Division
1	6 + 2 = 8	6 − 2 = 4	6 x 2 = 12	6 ÷ 2 = 3

Player 1 says, "Six times two equals twelve," and takes the 12 out of his number line.

> It is important that players verbalize their equations. A rule can be added that if the equation is not given, the player may not take out a card on that turn.

Player 2 rolls the dice and does the same.

If none of a player's equations equal a card still on the board, she must wait for her next roll of the dice without taking a card out of the number line.

The winner is either the first player to take out all thirteen cards or the one who has fewer cards in the number line when it is time to stop playing.

Questions

• Did your strategies at the end of the game change from those at the beginning of the game? Why? How?

• What would happen if you had multiplied instead of added?

• Which operation did you highlight the most?

• What will you do differently the next time you play this game?

Operation Bingo

The object of this game is to use at least two different operations (addition, subtraction, multiplication, or division) to create an equation whose answer allows a player to put a counter on the board. The goal of the game is to get three counters in a vertical, horizontal, or diagonal row.

Addition, subtraction, multiplication, and division

Grade 3
Grade 4
Grade 5

Two players

Materials

- ten-frame cards 1–6, four of each; the same if using a standard deck

- operation cards (page 166)

- counters of a different color or kind for each player

- paper

- pencils

- "Operation Bingo" game board for every two players

1	2	3	4	5
6	7	8	9	10
11	12	13	14	15
16	17	18	19	20

The cards are shuffled and stacked facedown. Player 1 takes five cards. Using the numbers on at least three of the cards plus the operation cards, Player 1 must make an equation using at least two different operations (addition, subtraction, multiplication, or division) that equals one of the numbers on the game board. If Player 2 agrees that Player 1 has created a valid equation, Player 1 places a counter on that number on the game board. All five cards are put in a discard pile.

Example

Player 1 takes five cards—4, 4, 3, 5, and 2. She makes the equation (4 x 4) + (5 – 2) = 19. Player 2 checks the equation for accuracy. Player 1 places a counter on 19.

Player 2 draws five cards and proceeds in the same manner.

When all the facedown cards have been used, the discard pile is shuffled, stacked facedown, and play continues until one player has three markers in a vertical, horizontal, or diagonal row.

Questions

- What strategies did you find helpful while playing this game?

- How did you decide which operations to use with which numbers?

- Were your strategies different when dealing with the smaller numbers as opposed to the larger numbers?

Variation 1: The game is played in exactly the same way, but the goal of the game is to have four markers in a row.

Variation 2: The game is played in exactly the same way, but cards 7 to 10 are added to the stack.

Variation 3: The game is played in exactly the same way with cards 1 to 6 or 1 to 10, but create a new game board with higher numbers.

Next-Door Neighbors

The game's goal is to color in squares that touch as many sides or corners of other colored squares. Players must use two different operations (addition, subtraction, multiplication, or division) to create a new number.

Addition, subtraction, multiplication, and division

Grade 3
Grade 4
Grade 5

Two players

Materials

- ten-frame cards 1–7, four of each; the same if using a standard deck

- operation cards (page 166)

- different color crayon for each player

- paper

- pencils

- "Next-Door Neighbors" game board for each player

1	2	3	4	5	6
7	8	9	10	11	12
13	14	15	16	17	18
19	20	21	22	23	24
25	26	27	28	29	30
31	32	33	34	35	36
37	38	39	40	41	42

- "Next-Door Neighbors" recording sheet for each player

Turn	Three Numbers	Equations	Points
1			
2			
3			
4			
5			
6			
7			
8			
9			
10			

How to play

The game is played for a predetermined amount of time or number of points. The cards are shuffled and stacked facedown.

Player 1 takes three cards from the stack. He writes the numbers on his recording sheet, and then uses them to create two different equations using two different operations (addition, subtraction, multiplication, or division) that result in a number on his game board. Player 1 picks one of these equations and then colors in the number on his board. He explains to Player 2 what he did that allowed him to color in the number on his board. All three cards are put in a discard pile. Players score one point for each colored square their new number touches on any side or corner.

Example

Player 1 draws 3, 5, and 2 and writes the numbers on his recording sheet. He figures out the following equationss on his recording sheet:

5 x 3 = 15

15 + 2 = 17

Player 1 colors in 17 on his game board, and then explains to Player 2 what he did that allowed him to color in the 17. He puts his cards in the discard pile.

Player 2 draws three cards and proceeds in the same manner.

If a player cannot form equations that will result in an uncolored number on her game board, she places the cards in the discard pile and waits for her next turn.

When the cards in the facedown stack have all been used, the discard pile is shuffled, stacked facedown, and play continues.

At the end of the predetermined game session, the player with more points is the winner or, if playing to a target number of points, the player who accumulates the needed points first wins.

Questions

- What strategies did you find helpful while playing this game?
- How did you decide which operations to use with which numbers?
- Were your strategies different when dealing with the smaller numbers versus the larger ones?

Six = The Seventh

The goal of the game is to create as many equations as possible using six numbers to equal a seventh number. Players get the most points for equations that use all six numbers.

Addition, subtraction, multiplication, and division

Grade 3
Grade 4
Grade 5

Two players

Materials

- ten-frame cards, or standard deck with face cards removed
- paper
- pencils
- timer

How to play

The cards are shuffled. Player 1 turns over the top six cards for both players to see. He places the seventh card facedown. (Players take turns being the dealer.)

Each player writes down the six faceup numbers on his paper. The timer is set for three minutes; the seventh card is flipped over.

Players have three minutes to create and write down equations that use the first six numbers to equal the number on the seventh card. A number can be used only once in an equation unless there are two or more cards with the same number. All six numbers can be used in a new equation. When the three minutes are up, players check each other's equations for accuracy.

Example

The six faceup cards are 4, 9, 1, 2, 5, and 3. The seventh card is a 7. Below are a few of the possible equations:

$9 - 2 = 7$

$4 + 2 + 1 = 7$

$9 + 1 - 3 = 7$

$9 - (4 - 2) = 7$

$2 \times 3 + 1 = 7$

$(1 \times 9) - 2 = 7$

$(9 \times 1) + 2 - 4 = 7$

Scoring is as follows:

- Equations using two of the six numbers earn two points (e.g., $9 - 2 = 7$).
- Equations using three of the six numbers earn six points (e.g., $4 + 2 + 1 = 7$).
- Equations using four of the numbers earn ten points (e.g., $(9 \times 1) + 2 - 4 = 7$).
- Equations using five of the six numbers earn fifteen points.
- Equations using all six numbers earn twenty-five points.
- If a player makes a mistake, the player who finds the mistake gets twenty points and the player who made the mistake gets no points for that equation.

The highest score wins!

Questions

- What was easy? What was more difficult?
- Is there any way you could use those numbers to make a division equation? A multiplication equation?

Target—24

The goal of the game is to create an equation that equals 24.

Addition, subtraction, multiplication, and division

Grade 3
Grade 4
Grade 5

Four players

Materials

- ten-frame cards with 0s removed, or standard deck with face cards removed

- operation cards (page 166)

- pencils

- "Target—24" recording sheet for each player

Round	Six numbers	Equation	Points for Round
1			
2			
3			
4			
5			
6			
7			
8			
9			
10			

How to play

The cards are shuffled and stacked facedown. Player 1 turns over six cards for all to see. (Players take turns being the dealer.) Using any or all of these six cards, players have to create one equation that equals 24. The equation may include one or more operations (addition, subtraction, multiplication, or division). A number can be used only once in an equation unless there are two or more cards with the same number among the six cards.

When all the players have made an equation, players check each other's work for accuracy.

Scoring is as follows:

- One point for each number used (e.g., if a player uses four of the six numbers, that player gets four points.)

- One point for each different operation used (e.g., if a player uses multiplication and addition, that player scores two points.)

Example

Round	Six numbers	Equation	Points for Round
1	5, 7, 1, 9, 8 ,3	$(7 \times 1) + 9 + 8 = 24$	4 for numbers used 2 for different operations = 6 for round

At the beginning of each round the cards are shuffled and six new cards are laid out with which to make equations that equal 24.

At the end of ten rounds, the player with the most points is the winner.

Questions

- Using these same cards, is there any other way you could equal 24?

- Was there any one strategy or operation that was helpful in getting to 24?

- Would this strategy work the same way if your six numbers were different? Greater? Smaller? Prove it.

Variation: The game is played in a similar manner, but the target number is changed or the number of cards laid out is increased or decreased.

The Games

The Elevator Game

The goal of this game is to make equations using as many numbers and different operations (addition, subtraction, multiplication, and division) as possible.

Addition, subtraction, multiplication, and division

Grade 3
Grade 4
Grade 5

Two players

Materials

- ten-frame cards, or standard deck with face cards removed

- operation cards (page 166)

- paper

- pencils

- "The Elevator Game" recording sheet for each player

Floor	Equation	Score
Tenth floor	= 10	
Ninth floor	= 9	
Eighth floor	= 8	
Seventh floor	= 7	
Sixth floor	= 6	
Fifth floor	= 5	
Fourth floor	= 4	
Third floor	= 3	
Second floor	= 2	
First floor	= 1	
		Total score

How to play

The cards are shuffled. Each player gets ten cards; they are placed faceup. The remaining cards are stacked facedown. Players use their ten cards to make an equation that equals 1, and then record it on the "first floor" line. A number can only be used once in an equation unless there are two or more cards with the same number among the ten cards.

Players check each other's work for accuracy.

Cards used for the first equation are put in a discard pile. Each player takes enough cards from the facedown stack to have ten cards again. (Players always have ten cards with which to make an equation.) Players continue in the same manner, making equations for each of the remaining floors in order.

When the cards in the facedown stack have all been used, the cards in the discard pile are shuffled, stacked facedown, and play continues.

Scoring is as follows:

- one point for every number used
- two points for use of addition
- four points for use of subtraction
- ten points for use of multiplication
- twenty points for use of division

Example

Floors	Equation	Score
Fifth floor	$(4 \times 5 - 8) \div 4 + 2 = 5$	5 for using five numbers 36 for using all four operations Total points = 41

After the lines for each floor have been filled, the player with more points wins.

Questions

- Convince me that your equation works.
- Could you have made an equation for that floor any other way using different or more operations or numbers?

The Add-to-It Equation Game

The goal of this game is to create and enlarge equations.

Addition, subtraction, multiplication, and division

Grade 3
Grade 4
Grade 5

Two players

Materials

- ten-frame cards, or standard deck with face cards removed

- operation cards (page 166)

- paper

- pencils

How to play

Players sit side by side, not across from each other. The cards are shuffled and stacked facedown.

Player 1 takes ten cards. Using these numbers and the operation cards, she makes a simple equation with three of the numbers. Player 1 gives Player 2 the remaining seven cards. Player 2 may not alter the operation or numbers of the original equation. Player 2 works on the original equation, using as many of the remaining seven cards and operation cards as he can. He may change one or both sides of the original equation as long as the left side of the equation equals the right side when he completes his equation.

Example

Player 1 picks card numbers 4, 6, 1, 5, 3, 1, 8, 2, 9, and 5. She makes the simple equation $4 + 1 = 5$.

Player 2 looks at the $4 + 1 = 5$ and extends it to $(4 + 1) \times 3 = 5 + 8 + 2$.

If the new equation is balanced, Player 2 gets a point for each of the number cards used. For instance, in the example above, Player 2 used six cards; he would get six points; Player 1 would get no points. If the new equation is wrong, players work together to correct it, but only Player 1 receives points for the numbers appropriately used in the first equation. Using the example above, Player 1 would get three points.

The ten cards used in the round are returned to the deck, and the cards are shuffled. Player 2 takes ten cards and starts the next round by making a simple equation.

Players continue to alternate roles until ten rounds have been played. The player with more points wins the game.

Questions

- What did you discover or decide while playing this game?

- Looking at those ten cards, is there any way you could incorporate division?

Multiple Operations Target

Players create equations using as many of their six cards and as many different operations (addition, subtraction, multiplication, and division) as possible.

Addition, subtraction, multiplication, and division

Grade 3
Grade 4
Grade 5

Two players

Materials

- timer

- pencils

- ten-frame cards, or standard deck with face cards removed

- operation cards (page 166)

- "Multiple Operations Target" recording sheet for each player

Round	Target Number	Equation	Points for Numbers Used	Points for Operations Used	Points for Round
1					
2					
3					
4					
5					
6					

Total points for game _____

How to play

Each round is played for a specific amount of time, for example, two minutes. The cards are shuffled and dealt. Each player receives six cards. Players will use their six cards throughout the game. Players lay the cards faceup. The remaining cards are stacked facedown.

Player 1 turns over the top card of the facedown stack. This is the target number. The timer is set. Players use their six cards and the operation cards to make an equation that equals the target number.

Players must use at least two of their cards to equal the target number. Cards may be used only once per round. A number can only be used once in an equation unless there are two or more cards with the same number among the six cards. All six cards can be used again in the next round.

When the timer goes off, the children stop. Players check each other's equations for accuracy. If the equation is correct, a player scores points on the basis of how many of the six cards and how many different operations (addition, subtraction, multiplication, and division) were used.

Scoring is as follows:

- One point for each of the six numbers used

- Two points for the use of addition

- Five points for the use of subtraction

- Ten points for the use of multiplication

- Twenty points for the use of division

Example

Player 1's cards are 0, 4, 9, 5, 3, and 2. For round 1 she records the following:

Round	Target Number	Equation	Points for Numbers Used	Points for Operations Used	Points for Round
1	7	$(9 - 5) + 3 + 0 = 7$	4	7	11

Each timed round begins by turning over a new target number. Players continue to use the same six cards dealt to them. The game is played for six rounds. The player with more points wins the game.

Questions

- Convince me that your equation equals the target number.

- Is there any way you could have used multiplication or division in that equation?

- Were there any target numbers that were easier or harder to make than others? Why do you think that was?

Variation 1: The game is played in the same way, but two cards are turned over from the facedown stack and then added together to form the target number.

Variation 2: The game is played in a similar manner but the players receive ten cards each. Two cards from the facedown stack are turned over and then multiplied to make the target number. Players must use at least three of their ten cards to make the target equation.

The Challenge

The goal of the game is to use as many of the ten numbers and as many operations (addition, subtraction, multiplication, and division) as possible to create an equation that equals the challenge number.

Addition, subtraction, multiplication, and division

Grade 3
Grade 4
Grade 5

Two players

Materials

- timer
- pencils
- ten-frame cards with 0s removed,
  or standard deck with face cards removed
- operation cards (page 166)
- "The Challenge" recording sheet for each player

Round	Challenge Number	Equation	Points for Numbers Used	Points for Operations Used	Points for Round
1					
2					
3					
4					
5					

Total points for game _____

How to play

The game is played for five rounds; each round is played for a predetermined amount of time, for example, two minutes. The cards are shuffled and ten cards are dealt to each player. (The players take turns being the dealer.) Players do not reveal their cards until the challenge is made.

Player 1 picks a number between 1 and 100 and says, "I challenge players to make an equation that equals ____ (any number she chooses)." This is the challenge number. The timer is set.

Players use their ten cards and the operation cards to make an equation that equals the challenge number. Each card may be used only once in the equation. Cards may not be combined to make a two-digit number (e.g., a 4 and a 9 may not be joined to make 49 or 94).

When the timer goes off, players stop work. Players then check each other's equations to make sure that they are valid equations and that they equal the challenge number.

Scoring is as follows:

- One point for each of the ten numbers used
- Two points for the use of addition
- Five points for the use of subtraction
- Ten points for the use of multiplication
- Twenty points for the use of division

Example

The challenge number is 50. Player 1's cards are 6, 3, 7, 9, 1, 6, 3, 4, 8, and 1. She writes the following on her recoding sheet:

Round	Challenge Number	Equation	Points for Numbers Used	Points for Operations Used	Points for Round
1	50	(6 x 7) + (9 – 1) = 50	4	17	21

The used cards are returned to the deck; the cards are shuffled and dealt for the new round. Player 2 chooses a new challenge number. (Players take turns selecting the challenge number.)

After five rounds of play, players total their points. The player with more points wins the game.

Questions

- What have you concluded after playing several rounds of this game?
- What strategy was helpful?
- Will that strategy work no matter what numbers you use?

The Operation Game

The goal of this game is to use as many operations (addition, subtraction, multiplication, and division) as possible to build an equation.

Addition, subtraction, multiplication, and division

Grade 3
Grade 4
Grade 5

Two players

Materials

- ten-frame cards with 0s removed, or standard deck with face cards removed

- operation cards (page 166)

- paper

- pencils

How to play

The game is played for a predetermined amount of time or number of points. The cards are shuffled and ten cards are dealt to each player. (Players take turns being the dealer.) Players lay their cards faceup and pick one card to be the START number and one card to be the FINISH number. Players use as many of the remaining eight cards as they can to get from the start number to the finish number. Scores are based on the number and type of operation cards used from start to finish.

Scoring is as follows:

- Addition: two points for every operation card used

- Subtraction: five points for every operation card used

- Multiplication: ten points for every operation card used

- Division: fifteen points for every operation card used

Example

Player 1 looks at her ten cards, (9, 2, 3, 5, 1, 3, 6, 8, 4, 7) and chooses 6 as the START number and 3 as the FINISH number. She writes the following steps on her paper:

START	6	
	+	8
14	÷	2
7	x	3
21	÷	7
FINISH	3	

Player 1's score:

- *One addition operation card = 2 points*
- *Two division operation cards = 30 points*
- *One multiplication operation card = 10 points*
- *42 total points earned for the round*

Players exchange papers and check each other's steps for accuracy. If a player makes an error, that player must correct it, and loses ten points from her score. The player who found the error gets ten points added to his score.

At the end of the predetermined game session, the player with more points is the winner, or if playing to a target number of points, the player who accumulates the needed points first wins.

Questions

- What did you discover while playing this game?
- Were some hands of ten cards harder to work with than others? Why was that?

Fractions

Introduction

Fractions Glossary 199

Comparing Fractions

Fraction Kit 200

Cover 202

Uncover 203

Fraction War 204

The Constant Denominator 204

The Constant Numerator 205

You Choose the Constant Denominator 205

You Choose the Constant Numerator 205

Fraction Feud 205

Denominator or Numerator? 205

Which Is Closer to 1? 206

Fraction More 208

Equivalent Fractions Concentration 210

Adding Fractions

Fraction Race 212

Different Denominators Fraction Race 213

Fraction Sums 214

Triple Fraction Sums 215

It Adds Up to 1 216

It Adds Up to $1\frac{1}{4}$ 216

Subtracting Fractions

Subtraction Fraction Race 213

Fraction Subtraction 215

Multiplying Fractions

Multiplying Fractions War 217

Introduction

The Common Core State Standards for Mathematics introduces fractions in the third grade (NGA Center and CCSSO 2010, p. 24, 3.NF).

Once they get the hang of them, children like fractions. No, … really! The challenge is that many students don't have opportunities to build a solid foundation with fractions. Then, as they progress through school without this basic understanding, fractions become a source of fear and dread. I call it fraction phobia. And yet we use fractions all the time in our real adult lives, both at home and at work. Fractions are important!

How can we help children with fraction phobia?

First, there is a school and community culture that sends children the message that fractions are hard. Whether intentionally or not, parents and teachers often relay the feeling that working with fractions is difficult. The majority of students come to middle school with little or no confidence in their abilities to work with fractions.

A great deal of the problem stems from the fact that children have little or no conceptual understanding of fractions. A good place to begin is with concrete experiences. Use "equal sharing" and real objects to introduce and reinforce the concept of fractions. Here are a few suggestions to get started:

- I have one brownie and the two of you will be sharing it equally. How much brownie will each of you get?

- I have one brownie and the five of you will be sharing it equally. How much brownie will each of you get?

- I have three brownies and the four of you will be sharing them equally. How much brownie will each of you get?

Next, introduce representational thinking by having children draw pictures to further help their understanding of the concept. Below are a few sample situations:

- Four children want to share a candy bar so that each child gets the same amount. How much of the candy bar should each child get? Draw a picture.

- I have one pizza to share with four people and I want everyone to get the same amount. Draw a picture to show how much each person gets.

- There are five apples, and I want to share them equally with four children. Draw a picture to show how much each child gets.

As you might expect, I strongly believe that fraction games can help children avoid or overcome fraction phobia. Use these games to give children the benefit of starting off on the right foot or to sort out the misunderstandings of the past. I recommend that you begin by making the Fraction Kits and then play the two Fraction Kit games that follow. When the children are ready for other games, you'll find that some of them require fraction cards (see sample opposite). The templates for the cards are available on the National Council of Teachers of Mathematics More4U web page (www.nctm.org/more4u).

- Print the cards on card stock.

- Laminate them if possible. Most education supply stores have laminating machines. This really helps with longevity.

- Cut them apart and begin to play.

$\frac{1}{2}$	$\frac{1}{3}$	$\frac{2}{3}$	$\frac{1}{4}$	$\frac{2}{4}$
$\frac{3}{4}$	$\frac{1}{5}$	$\frac{2}{5}$	$\frac{3}{5}$	$\frac{4}{5}$
$\frac{1}{6}$	$\frac{2}{6}$	$\frac{3}{6}$	$\frac{4}{6}$	$\frac{5}{6}$
$\frac{1}{8}$	$\frac{2}{8}$	$\frac{3}{8}$	$\frac{4}{8}$	$\frac{5}{8}$

Or you may want to have children make their own fraction cards. Teachers and parents (and even some students) have often told me that making their own flash cards helped the children visualize and understand fractions. All that is needed are 3 x 5-inch index cards (they come in a variety of colors now) and black markers. When possible, pose a problem that the new fraction cards can help illustrate. For example, to create cards for eighths, tell the children that eight friends want to equally share a long chocolate bar. If the children lay out the eighths fraction cards in a line, they can "see" that the cards from 1/8 through 4/8 are half of the cards or 1/2 of the chocolate bar. It should also be evident that 8/8 is the whole candy bar or "1."

As an aside, let me say that children seem to understand fractions better when the line between the two numbers is a horizontal line rather than a diagonal one. Frankly, I'm not sure why that is, but my experience has led me to this conclusion. All the "Fractions" chapter materials on NCTM's More4U web page use a horizontal line for fractions.

Fractions Glossary

When playing any math games, it is important that the children become familiar with the correct math terminology for certain facts and concepts. In this section there are three words to consistently use when doing the activities and games in this section; their definitions are below.

Numerator is the top number of a fraction. It is the number of parts you have.

Denominator is the bottom number of a fraction. It is the number of parts into which the whole is divided.

Equivalent is an item that has the same value or amount as another item.

$$\frac{2}{4} = \frac{4}{8}$$

Here is a simple way to remember the fraction parts: If you forget, just think "down" for denominator.

$$\frac{\text{Numerator}}{\text{Denominator}}$$

Fraction Kit

I have used this activity and the games "Cover" and "Uncover" with third, fourth, and fifth graders with great success. They really help children understand the concept of fractions. It takes a little preparation beforehand to get ready for these two games, but it is well worth the time and effort. Be sure that the children do the work. It's a learning experience, too.

Make sure that you and the children have plenty of time to do this preliminary activity.

Comparing fractions

Grade 3: CCSS.3.NF.A.1
CCSS.3.NF.A.3
Grade 4: CCSS.4.NF.A.1
CCSS.4.NF.A.2
Grade 5

Materials

- one set 9 x 12-inch pieces of red, green, blue, and yellow construction paper for each child and the teacher

- scissors

- pencils

- black markers

While it may be tempting to hurry up and get to the games, don't rush the following activity.

1. Give each of the children one set of the construction paper and ask them what they notice about the four pieces. How are they alike?

> Among other observations, I hope that the children will notice that all four are the same size and shape—that the sheets of paper are *congruent*. Use the big word! What other objects around the home or classroom are congruent? (Paper plates and playing cards are good examples.)

2. Then show the red sheet of paper and tell them to set it aside. This red piece of paper will *never* be cut. It will act as the game board for both Fraction Kit games. This piece represents 1—the whole.

3. Take the blue sheet of paper and have the children carefully fold it in half short end to short end ("hamburger style"), open it up, and then carefully cut on the fold.

> The easiest way for the children to fold the paper is to have them lay the paper on their desks or a table, fold it in half so that the corners match exactly, and then crease the paper with one hand while holding the corners together with the other hand. Sometimes children need help, from either a peer or an adult.

- Ask them what they notice about these two pieces of paper in terms of each other. *Are these two pieces congruent?*

- Ask the children how many of these pieces fit exactly on the 1, the whole, the piece that will not be cut up.

- Have the children write 1/2 on both pieces of paper with the marker. Talk about what this means.

4. Take the green sheet of paper and have the children carefully fold it in half short end to short end ("hamburger style") and then in half again in the same direction. Ask them how many sections they will have on the inside when they open it up. *Were they right?* Have the children open up the green paper and carefully cut on the folds.

- Ask them what they notice about these four pieces in terms of each other. *Are these four pieces congruent? How many fit exactly on 1/2 ? How many fit exactly on the whole?*

- Have them mark 1/4 on each of the four pieces. *What does this mean?*

- If you have two 1/4s what do you have? Is there another way to say that?

5. Take the yellow sheet of paper and have the children carefully fold it in half "hamburger style," and then in half again in the same direction. They then fold the sheet in half a third time in the same direction. Ask them how many sections they will have on the inside when they open it up. *Were they right?* Have the children open up the sheet and carefully cut on the folds.

- Ask them what they notice about these eight pieces in terms of each other. How are they alike? *Are these eight pieces congruent? How many fit exactly on 1/4? 1/2? How many fit exactly on the 1, the whole?*

- Have them mark 1/8 on each of the eight pieces. Ask them what this means.

- If you have two 1/8 pieces, what do you have? Is there another way to say that?

Let the children explore their fraction pieces, and ask questions: What else do they notice when they compare them? How many fourths equal a half? How many eighths equal a fourth? Half?

Now you are ready to play the two Fraction Kit games!

Fractions

Cover

The goal of this game is to cover the "board" (the uncut sheet of construction paper) completely and exactly—no pieces should overlap each other or overhang the sides of the board.

Comparing fractions

Grade 3: CCSS.3.NF.A.1
CCSS.3.NF.A.3
Grade 4: CCSS.4.NF.A.1–NF.A.2
Grade 5

Two players

Materials

- one Fraction Kit for each player

- one custom fraction die*

  * Blank 1/2-inch wooden cubes are available at most education supply stores or online. Mark 1/2 on one face, 1/4 on two faces, and 1/8 on three faces with a permanent black-ink marker.

How to play

Players put their red board in front of them, with all their fraction pieces close at hand. Player 1 rolls the die and puts that fraction piece on his board.

Player 2 proceeds in the same manner.

If a player rolls a fraction that cannot fit on the board, he loses that turn.

Players alternate turns until one player covers her board completely and exactly, winning the game.

Questions

- What did you notice about playing the game?

- What are you hoping to roll because you have an empty space on your board?

- Will anything else fit?

- What are your chances of rolling a 1/2? 1/4? 1/8?

- When you play next time, is there anything that you will do differently?

- How would you describe what you have on your board at the end of this game?

Uncover

The goal of this game is to uncover the uncut red "board" completely and exactly.

Comparing fractions

Grade 3: CCSS.3.NF.A.1
CCSS.3.NF.A.3
Grade 4: CCSS.4.NF.A.1–NF.A.2
Grade 5

Two players

Materials

- one Fraction Kit for each player

- one custom fraction die*

  * Blank 1/2-inch wooden cubes are available at most education supply stores or online. Mark 1/2 on one face, 1/4 on two faces, and 1/8 on three faces with a permanent black-ink marker.

How to play

Players put their red board in front of them. Each player begins the game by covering his board exactly and completely using any fraction pieces he wishes.

Player 1 rolls the die and takes off the fraction piece indicated. Player 2 proceeds in the same manner. If a player rolls a fraction that she does not have on her board, she removes other fraction pieces whose sum equals the rolled fraction. If a player rolls a fraction he cannot remove from the board, the player loses his turn.

Example

Player 1 has 1/4, 1/4, 1/4, 1/8, and 1/8 on her board. She rolls a 1/2. She looks at her board and removes two 1/4 pieces, equaling 1/2.

> I never make any suggestions when children first start playing this game. For the first game or two, most of the children play as if they can only take off a fraction piece when that specific fraction is rolled, for example, a 1/2 piece when 1/2 is rolled. Eventually one of the children will ask if they can take off two 1/4s when a 1/2 is rolled. Instead of saying yes, I ask the child to demonstrate for all of us why this might be a possibility.

Players alternate turns until one player uncovers his board, winning the game.

Questions

- What did you discover while playing the game?

- I see you rolled a 1/2 but didn't have a 1/2 on your board. Could you have removed anything else?

- When you play next time, is there anything that you will do differently?

- What's the best way to cover your board before you begin the game?

Fractions

Fraction War

The goal of this game is to create a fraction with the greatest value. Once the children become familiar with the basic game, try playing one of the five variations. While the goal remains the same, the cards are used differently in each variation.

Comparing fractions

Grade 3: CCSS.3.NF.A.1
CCSS.3.NF.A.3
Grade 4: CCSS.4.NF.A.1
CCSS.4.NF.A.2
Grade 5

Two players

Materials

- ten-frame cards with 0s removed, or standard deck with face cards removed
- "Fraction War" game board for each player

- paper
- pencil

How to play

The cards are shuffled and stacked facedown. Each player takes two cards and creates a fraction. The player with the fraction of the greater value wins a point for that round. The used cards are placed in a discard pile. Players again take two cards each and proceed as before. When all the cards in the facedown stack have been drawn, the winner is the player with more points.

Questions

- How do you know your fraction is greater than the other player's?
- What would you do differently if you had to make the least fraction?
- What number would you have had to draw to make your fraction greater than your partner's?

Variation 1: "The Constant Numerator" is played in a similar way to "The Constant Denominator," but a 1 card is placed in the numerator position on the game board and remains in place until the end of the game. The remaining cards are shuffled and stacked facedown. Each player takes a card and places it in the denominator position. The player with the greater fraction wins the point for that round. Play continues until all the facedown cards have been drawn. The player with more points wins the game.

Variation 2: To play "You Choose the Constant Denominator," players choose a number between 2 and 10 to be the constant denominator. Each player places that number in the denominator position. Play proceeds as described in "The Constant Denominator."

Variation 3: To play "You Choose the Constant Numerator," players choose a number between 2 and 10 to be the constant numerator, and places that number in the numerator position. Play proceeds as described in "The Constant Numerator."

Variation 4: To play "Fraction Feud," the cards are shuffled and stacked facedown. Player 1 takes one card; that is the denominator. Player 2 does the same. Player 1 takes a second card; that is the numerator. Player 2 does the same. The player with the greater fraction wins the point for that round. When all the cards in the facedown stack have been drawn, the player with more points is the winner.

Variation 5: To play "Denominator or Numerator?" the cards are shuffled and stacked facedown. Player 1 takes one card and decides whether to put it in the denominator or numerator space on the game board. Once the card is placed, it cannot be moved. Player 2 does the same.

Player 1 takes a second card and places it in the open space. Player 2 does the same. The player with the greater fraction wins the point for that round. When all the cards in the facedown stack have been drawn, the player with more points is the winner of the game.

Which Is Closer to 1?

The object of this game is to find a fraction card closer to 1 than the other player's card.

Comparing fractions

Grade 3: CCSS.3.NF.A.1
CCSS.3.NF.A.3
Grade 4: CCSS.4.NF.A.1
CCSS.4.NF.A.2
Grade 5

Two players

Materials

- 20 fraction cards

$\frac{1}{2}$	$\frac{1}{4}$	$\frac{2}{4}$	$\frac{3}{4}$	$\frac{4}{4}$
$\frac{1}{6}$	$\frac{2}{6}$	$\frac{3}{6}$	$\frac{4}{6}$	$\frac{5}{6}$
$\frac{6}{6}$	$\frac{1}{8}$	$\frac{2}{8}$	$\frac{3}{8}$	$\frac{4}{8}$
$\frac{5}{8}$	$\frac{6}{8}$	$\frac{7}{8}$	$\frac{8}{8}$	$\frac{1}{1}$

How to play

The cards are shuffled and stacked facedown. Player 1 draws a card and verbalizes the fraction; for example, "seven eighths." Player 2 turns over a card and also verbalizes her fraction; for example, "two fourths."

Because 7/8 is closer to 1 than 2/4, Player 1 takes both cards.

If both fractions are equal, for instance, 1/4 and 2/8, each player draws one more card and the fractions are compared. The player with the fraction closest to 1 takes all four cards.

Players alternate turns until all cards in the facedown stack have been drawn. The player with more cards wins the game.

Questions

- How did you figure out which fraction was closer to 1?

- How close to 1 is ____?

- Prove to me that ____ is closer to 1 than ____.

Variation 1: The game is played in the same way but the fraction cards from 1/12 through 12/12 are added to the deck.

Variation 2: The game is played in the same way, but the target number is the fraction 1/2.

Variation 3: The game is played in a similar manner; the target number can be 1 or 2. Players take two cards and add the fractions together to see which sum is closer to the target number.

Fraction More

The goal of this game is to have the greater fraction.

Comparing fractions

Grade 3: CCSS.3.NF.A.1
CCSS.3.NF.A.3
Grade 4: CCSS.4.NF.A.1
CCSS.4.NF.A.2
Grade 5

Two players

Materials

- fraction card deck

$\frac{1}{2}$	$\frac{1}{3}$	$\frac{2}{3}$	$\frac{1}{4}$	$\frac{2}{4}$
$\frac{3}{4}$	$\frac{1}{5}$	$\frac{2}{5}$	$\frac{3}{5}$	$\frac{4}{5}$
$\frac{1}{6}$	$\frac{2}{6}$	$\frac{3}{6}$	$\frac{4}{6}$	$\frac{5}{6}$
$\frac{1}{8}$	$\frac{2}{8}$	$\frac{3}{8}$	$\frac{4}{8}$	$\frac{5}{8}$
$\frac{6}{8}$	$\frac{7}{8}$	$\frac{1}{9}$	$\frac{2}{9}$	$\frac{3}{9}$
$\frac{4}{9}$	$\frac{5}{9}$	$\frac{6}{9}$	$\frac{7}{9}$	$\frac{8}{9}$
$\frac{1}{10}$	$\frac{2}{10}$	$\frac{3}{10}$	$\frac{4}{10}$	$\frac{5}{10}$
$\frac{6}{10}$	$\frac{7}{10}$	$\frac{8}{10}$	$\frac{9}{10}$	$\frac{1}{12}$
$\frac{2}{12}$	$\frac{3}{12}$	$\frac{4}{12}$	$\frac{5}{12}$	$\frac{6}{12}$
$\frac{7}{12}$	$\frac{8}{12}$	$\frac{9}{12}$	$\frac{10}{12}$	$\frac{11}{12}$
$\frac{1}{1}$	$\frac{2}{2}$	$\frac{3}{3}$	$\frac{4}{4}$	$\frac{6}{6}$
$\frac{8}{8}$	$\frac{10}{10}$	$\frac{12}{12}$	1	1

How to play

The cards are shuffled and dealt facedown to the players. (Players take turns being the dealer.) Players keep their cards in a facedown stack.

Players turn over their top card and compare their fractions. The player with the greater fraction takes both cards.

If players have fractions of equal value, for instance, 3/4 and 9/12, each player turns over one more card and the fractions are compared. The player with the greater fraction takes all four cards.

Play continues in this manner until all the cards in the players' facedown stacks have been drawn. The player with more cards wins.

Questions

- How do you know your fraction is greater than the other player's?

- Prove to me that _____ is a greater fraction than _____.

- Were there any fractions that were easier to compare? Why? Any fractions that were harder to compare? Why?

- What did you do to figure out which fraction was greater?

Variation: The game is played in a similar way, but the goal is to have the lesser fraction. That player takes all the cards for the round.

Fractions

Equivalent Fractions Concentration

The goal is to find as many equivalent fraction pairs of different fractions as possible.

Equivalent Fractions

Grade 3: CCSS.3.NF.A.1
CCSS.3.NF.A.3
Grade 4: CCSS.4.NF.A.1
CCSS.4.NF.A.2
Grade 5

Two players

Materials

- equivalent fraction cards

more**4**U

$\dfrac{2}{8}$	$\dfrac{1}{4}$	$\dfrac{4}{8}$	$\dfrac{1}{2}$
$\dfrac{6}{8}$	$\dfrac{3}{4}$	$\dfrac{8}{8}$	1
$\dfrac{2}{4}$	$\dfrac{1}{2}$	$\dfrac{4}{4}$	1
$\dfrac{2}{6}$	$\dfrac{1}{3}$	$\dfrac{3}{6}$	$\dfrac{1}{2}$
$\dfrac{4}{6}$	$\dfrac{3}{4}$	$\dfrac{6}{6}$	1
$\dfrac{5}{10}$	$\dfrac{1}{2}$	$\dfrac{10}{10}$	1

Pregame practice

The practice session with the cards *faceup* allows the children to see what they are expected to do mathematically.

The cards are shuffled and arranged faceup in a grid of six rows with four cards in each row. Player 1 looks for two fraction cards that are different but equivalent and then verbalizes both fractions. He takes both cards. Player 2 does the same.

Example

Player 1 matches 4/8 with 1/2. He says, "Four-eighths is equal to one-half," and takes both cards. Player 2 matches 2/8 and 1/4. She says, "Two-eighths is equal to one-fourth," and takes both cards.

Players alternate turns until all the cards have been matched.

How to play

The cards are shuffled and Player 1 arranges the fraction cards facedown in a grid of six rows with four cards in each row. (Players take turns being the dealer.)

Player 1 turns over one card, keeping it in place, and verbalizes the fraction and what he is looking for, for example; "Two-fourths. I am looking for another fraction that is equivalent to two-fourths."

Player 1 turns over another card, keeping it in place. If it is equivalent to the first fraction card, Player 1 takes both cards. If it is not equivalent, the cards are turned facedown in the same place. Player 2 proceeds in the same manner.

Players alternate turns until all possible matches have been made. Players count their cards. The player with more cards wins the game.

Questions

- You just turned over a _____. What are you looking for that would be equivalent?
- Is there anything else that would be equivalent?
- Prove to me that _____ is equivalent to _____.

Fraction Race

The goal is to create fractions with like denominators; then add and reduce them.

Adding fractions with like denominators
Reducing fractions
Variation 1: Subtracting fractions with like denominators
Variation 2: Adding fractions with different denominators

Grade 3
Grade 4: CCSS.4.NF.A.1
CCSS.4.NF.B.3b–3c
Grade 5: CCSS.5.NF.A1

Two players

Materials

- two dice

- ten-frame cards with 0s, 1s, and 2s removed,
  or standard deck with aces, 2s, and face cards removed

- pencils

- "Fraction Race" recording sheet for each player

Round	Denominator	Equation	Reduced	Points
1				
2				
3				
4				
5				
6				
7				
8				
9				
10				

How to play

The cards are shuffled and stacked facedown. Player 1 rolls the dice and adds the two numbers together to find the sum. The sum is the denominator that both players will use to begin the game. Player 1 turns over two cards from the stack. He uses these two numbers as numerators and creates two fractions.

Example

Player 1 rolls a 4 and a 3. He adds them together for the sum of 7. The number 7 is now the starting denominator of the game. Player 1 turns over cards 2 and 6, and creates 2/7 and 6/7.

Player 1 writes the two fractions on his recording sheet. He adds the two fractions and writes his answer; then he reduces it. Player 2 checks Player 1's work, and if Player 1 is correct, he gets one point. If he is not correct, he must correct it, but he does not get a point. Player 1 puts the two used cards into a discard pile.

Round	Denominator	Equation	Reduced	Points
1	7	$\frac{2}{7} + \frac{6}{7} = \frac{8}{7}$	$1\frac{1}{7}$	1

Player 2 takes two cards and proceeds in the same manner using the same denominator.

At the beginning of each round, players alternate turns rolling the dice to determine the new denominator for that round. Play continues as above for ten rounds. The player with more points is the winner.

Questions

- What was easy about this game? What was hard?
- Explain how you reduced _____ + _____ (for example, 7/4 + 4/4).

Variation 1: "Subtraction Fraction Race" is played in a similar manner, but the smaller fraction is subtracted from the greater fraction.

Variation 2: "Different Denominators Fraction Race" is played in a similar manner, but the numbers on each die are used so that players add fractions with two different denominators.

Fraction Sums

The goal of the game is to add and reduce fractions.

Adding fractions with like denominators
Variation 1: Adding three fractions
Variation 2: Subtracting fractions

Grade 3
Grade 4: CCSS.4.NF.A.1
CCSS.4.NF.B.3b–3c
Grade 5: CCSS.5.NF.A1

Two players

Materials

- paper
- pencils
- fraction addition cards (see sample below) more**4U**

1/2 + 1/2	1/3 + 1/3	1/3 + 2/3	2/3 + 2/3	1/4 + 1/4	1/4 + 3/4	3/4 + 3/4
1/5 + 1/5	2/5 + 3/5	1/5 + 4/5	2/5 + 4/5	3/5 + 3/5	3/5 + 4/5	4/5 + 4/5
1/6 + 1/6	1/6 + 5/6	5/6 + 5/6	1/8 + 1/8	1/8 + 3/8	1/8 + 5/8	1/8 + 7/8
3/8 + 3/8	3/8 + 5/8	5/8 + 5/8	5/8 + 7/8	7/8 + 7/8	1/9 + 2/9	1/9 + 5/9
2/9 + 4/9	2/9 + 7/9	4/9 + 5/9	4/9 + 8/9	5/9 + 7/9	7/9 + 8/9	1/10 + 3/10
1/10 + 9/10	3/10 + 7/10	3/10 + 9/10	7/10 + 9/10	10/10 + 10/10		

How to play

The fraction addition cards are shuffled and stacked facedown. Player 1 takes the top card and reads it aloud. She lays it faceup for the Player 2 to see.

Both players write this fraction addition on their papers, add it, and reduce it. Players compare and defend their sums. Each player with the correct sum receives one point.

Example

Player 1 turns over 5/8 + 5/8. Both players write it on their papers and add the fractions together to get 10/8. They reduce it to $1\frac{2}{8}$, and then reduce it again to $1\frac{1}{4}$.

Player 2 turns over the next fraction addition card and the play proceeds in the same manner.

Players alternate turns drawing cards. When all the fraction addition cards have been drawn, the player with more points is the winner of the game.

Questions

- What did you discover while playing this game?

- Prove to me that _____ + _____ = _____.

- Did anything prove challenging while playing this game?

Variation 1: To play "Triple Fraction Sums," you will have to create cards for adding three fractions with like denominators (e.g., 2/8 + 3/8 + 9/8). The game is played in the same manner as "Fraction Sums."

Variation 2: "Fraction Subtraction" cards using like denominators (e.g., 12/8 – 2/8) are made; the object of the game is to subtract the fractions and then reduce the difference.

It Adds Up to 1

The goal is to cover three fractions that when added together have a sum exactly equal to 1.

Adding fractions with different denominators

Grade 3
Grade 4: CCSS.4.NF.A.1
CCSS.4.NF.B.3b–3c
Grade 5: CCSS.5.NF.A1

Two players

Materials

- different counters for each player
- "It Adds Up to 1" game board

$\dfrac{1}{4}$	$\dfrac{3}{8}$	$\dfrac{3}{8}$	$\dfrac{2}{8}$
$\dfrac{1}{8}$	$\dfrac{3}{8}$	$\dfrac{1}{2}$	$\dfrac{1}{8}$
$\dfrac{5}{8}$	$\dfrac{1}{4}$	$\dfrac{1}{8}$	$\dfrac{5}{8}$
$\dfrac{2}{8}$	$\dfrac{1}{8}$	$\dfrac{5}{8}$	$\dfrac{1}{4}$

How to play

Player 1 chooses any fraction square on the game board and covers it with one of her counters. Player 2 covers a different fraction square with one of his counters.

Players alternate turns. The first player to cover three squares that equal 1 exactly is the winner.

Questions

- What strategies helped you to cover fractions that equal 1?
- Convince me that your three fractions equal 1.

Variation: "It Adds Up to 1¼" is played in the same way. The winner is the first player to cover three fractions that exactly equal 1¼.

Multiplying Fractions War

The goal of this game is to multiply fractions and have the greatest product.

Multiplying fractions

Grade 4

Grade 5

Two players

Materials

- ten-frame cards with 0s removed, or standard deck with face cards removed

- "Multiplying Fractions" game board for each player

Numerator   Numerator

—————— x ——————

Denominator   Denominator

How to play

The cards are shuffled and stacked facedown. Player 1 takes the top card and places it on any one of the four positions. **Once the card is placed in position, the number cannot be moved to a different space.** Player 2 takes a card and does the same. Players continue to alternate taking a card until both players have a card in all four positions on their game boards.

Players then multiply their two fractions, simplify (reduce) them, and find a product. Players check each other's work for accuracy.

The player with the greater fraction wins.

> If you are a parent who hasn't multiplied fractions lately, here's a short tutorial:
> 1/2 x 2/5
> Multiply the numerators: 1 x 2 =2
> Multiply the denominators: 2 x 5 = 10
> The product is 2/10.
> Reduce 2/10 to 1/5.

Questions

- Did you find a strategy that helped you get the greater fraction? What is it?

- If you had the opportunity to change these four numbers around, what would you do? Would that give you a greater product?

- Where did you put your greatest numbers? Lesser numbers?

- What will you do differently the next time you play this game?

Variation: The game is played in a similar manner, but the goal of the game is to have the product with the lesser fraction.

The Games

Decimals

Introduction

Comparing Decimals to Tenths

Who Is Closer to One-Half? 221

Comparing Decimals to Hundredths

More Who Is Closer to One-Half? 222

Decimal Winner Takes All 223

Read Me Your Number 225

Comparing Decimals to Thousandths

Thousandths Decimal Winner Takes All 224

Adding and Comparing Decimals

Decimal Dice 227

Decimal Dice 2 229

Decimal Race to 500 231

Decimal Race to 1,000 232

Subtracting and Comparing Decimals

Close to 0 233

Three-Card Close to 0 233

Comparing, Adding, and Subtracting Decimals

Decimal Riddles 234

Multiplying and Comparing Decimals

Target—3 236

Target—1 238

Introduction

According to the *Common Core State Standards for Mathematics* (NGA Center and CCSSO 2010, p.31), by the end of fourth grade students should "understand notation for fractions, and compare decimal fractions."

It's important that children gain a firm understanding of decimals because they appear all around us on a daily basis. A few of the situations in which we encounter decimals are when we—

- pay for goods;
- fill the car with gas;
- calculate mileage;
- look at batting averages;
- write checks and balance the checkbook;
- read the nutritional or ingredient information on food, toothpaste, medicine, and other products;
- step on a digital scale; and
- take measurements.

Our decimal system gives us the flexibility to write numbers as large or as small as we like. The keystone to the decimal system is the decimal point. Anything on the left of the decimal point represents a whole number, anything on the right of the decimal represents a value less than one (similar to a fraction). Moving from left to right, the value of each place on the right of the decimal point is one-tenth the value of the place immediately on the left.

whole number	tenths	hundredths	thousandths
____ .	____	____	____

The following decimal games will help children gain understanding when comparing, adding, and subtracting decimals.

Who Is Closer to One-Half?

In this game, each ten-frame card represents a tenth decimal value. The goal is to have a decimal value closer to one-half.

Comparing decimals to tenths
Variation: Comparing decimals to hundredths

Grade 4: CCSS.4.NF.C.7
Grade 5

Two players

Materials

- ten-frame cards with 0s and 10s removed, or standard deck with 10s and face cards removed

- "Who Is Closer to One-Half?" game board for each player

0.___

(tenths)

> The game board helps the children visualize the decimal.

How to play

The cards are shuffled and stacked facedown. Each player takes one card from the top of the stack and places it faceup on his game board. The players read their decimals to each other. The player with the decimal closer to one-half wins the round and takes both cards.

Example

Player 1 turns over an 8 and says, "eight tenths." Player 2 turns over a 4 and says, "four tenths." Four-tenths is closer to one-half, so Player 2 takes both cards.

> Be careful to use the correct language when reading decimals out loud. Always say the word "tenths" rather than "zero point"; for instance, "eight tenths" not "zero point eight."

If both players have values equidistant from one-half, a tie is declared.

To break the tie, each player draws a second card and puts it faceup on top of the first card. The player whose tenth value is closer to one-half takes all four cards.

Play continues until all the cards in the facedown stack have been drawn. The winner is the player with more cards.

Questions

- Convince me that your value is closer to one-half than the other player's.

- How close to one-half are you? How did you figure it out?

Variation: "More 'Who Is Closer to One-Half?'" is played in a similar manner, but each player takes two cards and creates a value of hundredths that is as close to one-half as possible. For example, Player 1 draws a 6 and a 3. The player can make .63 or .36.

0 ._____   _____

   (tenths)   (hundredths)

Decimal Winner Takes All

The goal of this game is to create the greatest decimal possible.

Comparing decimals to hundredths
Variation: Comparing decimals to thousandths

Grade 4: CCSS.4.NF.C.7
Grade 5

Two players

Materials

- ten-frame cards with 10s removed, or
  standard deck with 10s and face cards removed

- "Decimal Winner Takes All" game board for each player

> 0. _____ _____
>   (tenths) (hundredths)

How to play

The cards are shuffled and stacked facedown. Player 1 takes one card. He places it faceup on the tenth or hundredth place as he chooses. It must be in place on the board before Player 2 can take her turn. **Once the card is placed in position, it cannot be moved to a different space.** Player 2 takes one card and proceeds in the same manner.

Player 1 takes a second card and turns it over, placing it on the empty space. Player 2 does the same. Players read their decimal values to each other.

Example: Player 1's first card is a 6. He places it on the tenths space of his game board. His second card is a 4, and he puts it on the hundredths space of his game board for 0.64. He says, "I have sixty-four hundredths."

> Be very careful to model the correct language when reading decimals out loud. Always use the word "hundredths" rather than "zero point"; for instance, "sixty-four hundredths" not "zero point six four."

Players compare their decimals and decide which player has the greater decimal. The player with the greater decimal takes all four cards.

Play continues until all the facedown cards have been drawn. The winner is the player with more cards.

Questions

- Did you find a strategy to help you make the greatest decimal possible?

- Can you prove to me that _____ is greater than _____?

- I see you have your tenths line open. What number are you hoping for? What are your chances of getting that number?

Variation: "Thousandths Decimal Winner Takes All" is played in a similar manner, but players each take three cards and create the greatest possible value of thousandths.

0.	_____	_____	_____
	(tenths)	(hundredths)	(thousandths)

Read Me Your Number

The goal of this game is to create the greatest decimal number possible.

Comparing decimals to hundredths

Grade 4: CCSS.4.NF.C.7

Grade 5

Two players

Materials

- ten-frame cards with 10s removed, or
  standard deck with 10s and face cards removed

- pencils

- "Read Me Your Number" recording sheet for each player

Round	1,000	100	10	1	0.1	0.01	Final Number
1							
2							
3							
4							
5							
6							
7							
8							
9							
10							

How to play

The cards are shuffled and stacked facedown. Player 1 draws a card and places it faceup for Player 2 to see. Both players must immediately write this number down on any place value position they choose on the Round 1 line of their game board. **Once the number is written down, it cannot be changed to a different place value position.**

Player 2 draws a card and places it faceup for Player 1 to see. As before, both players immediately write this number down on their game boards. Players continue to alternate drawing cards until all six place-value positions for round 1 are filled.

Players compare their numbers and read them aloud to each other.

Example

Player 1 has written on his recording sheet—

Round	1,000	100	10	1	0.1	0.01	Final Number
1	7 (7,000)	8 (800)	4 (40)	2	5 (.5)	3 (.03)	7,842.53

Player 1 reads his number to the other player saying, "Seven thousand, eight hundred, forty-two, and fifty-three hundredths."

The player with the greater number earns ten points for that round. At the end of ten rounds, the player with more points wins the game.

Questions

- At the end of round 1 ask, "Is there anything you will do differently in the next round?"

- What strategies have you discovered to be helpful in creating the largest possible number?

- What number are you hoping for? What are the chances that you will draw a ___?

Decimal Dice

The object of the game is to add decimal numbers in order to have the greatest sum possible after ten turns.

Adding Decimals

Grade 4
Grade 5: CCSS.NBT.B.7

Two players

Materials

- one die

- pencils

- "Decimal Dice" recording sheet for each player

Turn	Whole number	Tenths value	Total
1			
2			
3			
4			
5			
6			
7			
8			
9			
10			
			Sum

How to play

Player 1 rolls the die. The number rolled is the whole number. Player 1 writes the whole number on her recording sheet. She rolls the die a second time, and that number is the tenths value. She writes in the tenths value, and then the total number. She reads it aloud to Player 2.

Example

Player 1's first roll is a 2; the second is a 6. She writes 2.6 on her recording sheet and reads the decimal number aloud.

Turn	Whole number	Tenths value	Total
1	2	.6	2.6

Player 2 proceeds in the same manner.

Players alternate rolling the dice until each player has had ten turns. Players add their ten total numbers together, exchange papers, and check each other's addition for accuracy. The player with the greater sum wins the game.

Questions

- Was there any strategy involved in this game?

- Looking back at each turn, what helped you have the greater sum?

Variation: The game is played in the same way, but rather than using a die, numbers are determined using ten-frame cards 1 to 9. Cards are shuffled and stacked facedown. Players draw two cards, one at a time. The first card is the whole number; the second is the decimal. Used cards are placed in a discard pile. When the facedown stack is depleted, the discard pile is shuffled and stacked, and play continues.

Decimal Dice 2

The goal of the game is to get as close to 10 as possible in three rounds of play. Players must complete three rounds no matter how close they might be to 10. This is not an "exact" game, so the sum may be over 10.

Adding decimals

Grade 4
Grade 5: CCSS.NBT.B.7

Two players

Materials

- two dice

- pencils

- "Decimal Dice 2" recording sheet for each player

Round 1:	____ . ____
Round 2:	____ . ____
Round 3:	____ . ____
Sum:	____ . ____

How to play

Player 1 rolls both dice. She must decide which number will be the whole number and which will be the decimal.

Example

Player 1 rolls a 2 and a 6. She can make either 2.6 or 6.2.

Player 1 records the number on her recording sheet for round 1.

Player 2 rolls both dice and proceeds in the same manner.

Players alternate turns until each player has completed three rounds. Players add their numbers, and exchange papers to check each other's addition for accuracy. The player with the sum closest to 10 wins the round and earns one point.

Example

Player 1's final sum is 9.4. Player 2's final sum is 10.2. Player 2's sum is closest to 10, so Player 2 wins one point.

After ten rounds, the player with the most points wins the game.

Questions

- What is your strategy for getting as close to 10 as you can?
- How close to 10 are you?
- How did you figure out how close to 10 you are?
- Convince me that you are closer to 10 than the other player.

Decimal Race to 500

The goal of the game is to be the first player whose sum equals 500. This is not an "exact" game so the sum may be more than 500.

Adding decimals

Grade 4
Grade 5: CCSS.NBT.B.7

Two players

Materials

- ten-frame cards with 10s removed, or standard deck with 10s and face cards removed

- paper

- pencils

How to play

Three-digit numbers are made according to the following rules:

- Even numbers are whole numbers.
- Odd numbers are decimals.

The cards are shuffled and stacked facedown. Player 1 draws three cards and arranges them any way he wants, following the odd-even rules. He writes the number at the top of his paper, and verbalizes the number to Player 2.

Example

Player 1 draws 7, 4, and 9. He can make 4.79 or 4.97. He chooses 4.97 and writes it at the top of his paper. He says to Player 2, "My number is four and ninety-seven hundredths."

Player 2 draws three cards and proceeds in the same manner.

Player 1 takes his second turn and proceeds in the same manner, but he adds the second number to his first number.

Example

Continuing the above example, Player 1 draws 6, 2, and 5. He can make 62.5 or 26.5. He writes 62.5 on his paper and adds it to his first number. He says to Player 2, "My number is sixty-two and five tenths. The sum of all my numbers is sixty-seven and forty-seven hundredths."

$$\begin{array}{r} 4.97 \\ + 62.5 \\ \hline 67.47 \end{array}$$

Players continue to alternate turns until one player has a winning sum equaling 500 or more.

Questions

- What numbers are you hoping to draw? Why?

- How close to 500 are you? How did you figure it out?

- What was easy about this game? Difficult?

- Can you think of a way to change this game so it is easier or more challenging?

Variation: "Decimal Race to 1,000" is played exactly the same way, but the goal is to be the first player whose sum equals 1,000. This game might be played over several days.

Close to 0

The goal of this game is to be the player with a difference closer to 0 after ten turns.

Subtracting decimals

Grade 4
Grade 5: CCSS.NBT.B.7

Two players

Materials

- ten-frame cards with 10s removed, or a standard deck with 10s and face cards removed

- paper

- pencils

How to play

The cards are shuffled and stacked facedown. Both players write 100 at the top of their papers.

Player 1 draws one card; this card is the whole number. She takes a second card; this is the tenth-place decimal.

Example

Player 1 draws a 7 and a 4. She writes 7.4 under 100 on her paper, and subtracts it from 100.

Player 2 checks Player 1's subtraction for accuracy, and Player 1 puts her cards in a discard pile.

Player 2 draws two cards and play proceeds in the same manner. (When the cards in the facedown stack have all been used, the discard pile is shuffled, stacked, and play continues.)

Players alternate turns until each player has had ten turns. The player whose final difference is the lesser (closer to zero) wins the game.

Questions

- How far from zero is your number? How did you figure it out?

- What was the most difficult part of playing this game?

- What numbers were you hoping to draw for the whole number? Why?

- Did it matter what number you drew for the decimal? Why?

Variation: "Three-Card Close to Zero" is played in a similar manner with players drawing three cards at each turn. The first card is the whole number; the second card is the tenths value; and the third card is the hundredths value. The number is subtracted from 100.

Decimal Riddles

Players try to correctly answer as many riddles as possible.

Comparing, adding, and subtracting decimals

Grade 4: CCSS.4.NF.C.7
Grade 5: CCSS.NBT.B.7

Two or more players

Materials

- paper
- pencils
- "Decimal Riddles" worksheet for each player

Decimal Riddles

Name _____

I have 4 ones, 6 tenths, and 7 hundredths. What is my number?

I have 3 ones, 12 tenths, and 4 hundredths. What is my number?

I have 2 ones, 14 hundredths, and 3 tenths. What is my number?

I have 2 ones, 16 tenths, and 12 hundredths. What is my number?

I have 40 hundredths and 5 tenths. What is my number?

I have 3 ones, 24 tenths, and 32 hundredths. What is my number?

> The riddles are provided as an introduction to the game. As children become familiar with the game and more adept at operations with decimal numbers, create new riddles, or let teams invent their own with which to challenge each other or the entire class.

How to play

When introducing this game to students, it might be helpful to play it with the whole class or group. Students are paired into teams. The first riddle is posed, and the children talk and work together in their team to solve it. The teacher decides how much time to allot for solving this first riddle. (As the riddles get more complex, more time may be needed.)

When time is up, the teacher asks for a team volunteer to explain and defend their answer to the riddle. A whole-class discussion should ensue. The teacher might ask a second team with a different answer to explain and defend why they think their answer is correct. When the correct answer is proved, teams with that answer get one point.

> Try to stay out of the conversation as much as possible. Guide it by asking questions, and only confirm the right answer at the very end of the discussion.

The game proceeds to the second riddle using the same process. When all the riddles have been answered, the team(s) with the most points is the winner.

At some point, to keep things interesting, have the children play the game against each other or in team against team. Another possibility is to hand out the complete worksheet of riddles, and let the children work on it for a predetermined amount of time. When time is up, players or teams compare and defend answers. They get one point for every correct answer. The player or team with the most points wins the game.

The game is easily adaptable for home play. Decide whether to pose the riddles one at a time or all at once. When the riddle has been figured out, ask your child to explain and defend his or her reasoning. Let your child do the talking. Ask questions, but don't confirm the right answer until the very end of the discussion.

Questions

- What did you do to help yourself while working on these riddles?
- What was easy? What was more difficult? What do you need to practice?

Target—3

The goal of this game is to be the closest to 3 after six rounds. Players must play six rounds no matter how close they might be to 3. This is not an "exact" game, so sums may be more than 3.

Multiplying decimals
Adding decimals

Grade 4
Grade 5: CCSS.NBT.B.7

Two players

Materials

- die
- paper
- pencils
- "Target—3" recording sheet for each player

Round	Number Rolled x .1, .2, .3, .4, or .5	Product
1	x	
2	x	
	Sum	
3	x	
	Sum	
4	x	
	Sum	
5	x	
	Sum	
6	x	
	Total Sum	

How to play

Player 1 rolls the die and then must decide by which decimal value—.1, .2, .3, .4, or .5—to multiply the number rolled so that he can be closer to 3 after playing six rounds. He writes the multiplication equation on his recording sheet.

Example

Player 1 rolls a 2, and decides to multiply that by .3. He records it as—

Round	Number Rolled x .1, .2, .3, .4, or .5	Product
1	2 x .3	.6

Player 2 checks Player 1's multiplication for accuracy. She then rolls the die and play proceeds in the same manner.

At the end of round 2, players add their products from rounds 1 and 2 to keep a running total of their sums.

After six rounds, the player whose sum is closer to 3 is the winner.

Example

At the end of six rounds, Player 1's total is 3.6; Player 2's total is 2.1. Player 1's sum is closer to 3 than player 2's, so Player 1 is the winner.

Questions

- After playing this game several times, have you developed any strategies that help you get as close to 3 as possible?

- How did you know you were the winner of the game?

- Who won? Player 1 who scored 3.1 or Player 2 who scored 2.9? Why?

- After five rounds your sum is 2.3 and you roll a 6. What should you multiply the 6 by to be close to 3? How do you know?

- If your running total after five rounds is 1.8 and you roll a 6, what should you multiply the 6 by to be close to 3? How do you know?

Variation: "Target—1" is played in a similar manner, but students multiply the number on the die by .01, .02, .03, .04, or .05. The player who is closer to 1 after six rounds wins.

Decimals

The Games

Money

Introduction

Adding and Trading Coins

    Race to $1.00 241

    Money Race 242

    73¢ 243

    How Much More to $1.00? 245

    $2.00 247

    $5.00 249

Big Money

    $1,000,000 251

Introduction

Even though debit, credit, and gift cards have become the standard method of exchange, children need to learn about money—coins and paper currency. They need to be able to count money and make change. I have often seen third, fourth, and fifth graders struggle to do one or the other or both.

The very best way for children to learn about money is to use the real thing!

Parents, consider giving your children a small allowance for those little extras children see and want. Part of learning is practicing. Let your children make the purchasing decisions with their own money. Let them pay for the gum or candy or toy that they want. Even if you don't agree with their spending choices, it's okay. By letting them learn from their mistakes when the stakes aren't high, they will be better money managers in the long run. And they'll gain experience counting out bills and coins and making change.

Teachers, I'm not talking about pictures of money in a workbook or plastic money that most schools use to teach money! No, I'm talking real pennies, nickels, dimes, and quarters and faux paper money for classroom use.

I discovered early in my teaching career that children will use that plastic stuff if they have to, but give them some real coins and interest and engagement soar!

But teachers are concerned about two issues:

1. Teachers spend money on their classrooms all the time. It's true that it is a hefty little investment to get enough pennies, nickels, dimes, and quarters for an entire class to play some of the following money games. (I invested about $80.00.) But that money will still be there the day you retire. The money you spent on crayons, borders, and other supplies will not. Think of it as a nest egg!

2. Most teachers worry that some children will "borrow" the coins. I learned that no matter the socioeconomic level of the children, a few children will "borrow." I sat my students down and told them I knew them well enough to know that they were good kids, and that I trusted them completely. Because of that trust, I was going to let them use some of my money. Only once in many years of teaching did I regret that trust. On the day I retired, I counted my nest egg, and discovered that I actually had more money than I had started with. Children would bring in money they found on the playground and put it in our stash!

So get some real coins, go to the local 99¢ store and buy faux paper money, and give some of the following games a try.

Race to $1.00

The goal of this game is to trade pennies, nickels, dimes, and quarters for a $1.00 bill.

Money

Grade 3
Grade 4
Grade 5

Two players

Materials

- ten-frame cards 1–6, four of each; the same if using a standard deck
- tub of pennies, nickels, dimes, and quarters
- one $1.00 bill

How to play

The cards are shuffled and stacked facedown. Player 1 draws a card and takes that many pennies. If he has enough pennies to trade for a nickel, he does so. When players have enough coins to "trade up" to the next coin value, they are expected to do so. Player 1 puts the card in a discard pile. Player 2 draws a card and proceeds in the same manner.

Players alternate turns until one player trades four quarters for a $1.00 bill and wins the game.

As the children become familiar with the game and more experienced with money, you will notice that when a child draws a 5, she will take a nickel instead of five pennies. This is good! She completely understands the value of a nickel. However, she must be able to explain to the other player why she can do this. Do not tell the children that they can do this. Let them discover it and share their discovery with the other children.

Questions

- You have two quarters, one dime, one nickel, and three pennies. How much is that worth?
- How much more money do you have than the other player?
- How close to $1.00 are you?
- I see you have three dimes. How much is that worth? How much is a quarter worth? What could you do to trade the three dimes for a quarter?

Variation 1: The game is played in the same way, but players must tell each other how much money they have after each turn.

Variation 2: The game is played the same way, but ten-frame cards 1 to 9 are used.

Variation 3: "Cut Throat" is played in a similar manner, but if a player fails to make a trade when he can do so, the other player gets the money from his most recent turn and adds it to her total.

Money Race

The goal of this game is to have the greater value in coins by the end of the game.

Money

Grade 3
Grade 4
Grade 5

Two players

Materials

- ten-frame cards 1–6, four of each; the same if using a standard deck
- tub of pennies, nickels, dimes, and quarters
- paper plate for each player and one for the "bank"

- "Money Race" action chart

Draw	Action
1	Choose any one coin from the bank
2	Subtract a penny
3	Subtract a nickel or 5 pennies
4	Subtract a dime or a combination of coins that equals 10¢
5	Subtract a quarter or a combination of coins that equals 25¢
6	Choose any one coin from the bank

How to play

Ten pennies, five nickels, four dimes, and one quarter, which equal $1.00, are placed on the bank's paper plate. Each player puts the same combination of coins on his paper plate. The cards are shuffled and stacked facedown.

Player 1 draws one card. He matches the card number to the number on the action chart and follows the instructions on the chart for that number, either choosing a coin from the bank and adding it to his money or subtracting coins from his money and putting them in the bank.

Player 2 selects a card and does the same.

Players continue in this manner until both have completed ten turns. Each player calculates the value of his coins. The player whose coins have the greater value wins the game.

Questions

- What is the value of all your coins at this very minute?
- How does the amount you have compare with the amount the other player has?
- If you traded that for pennies, how many pennies would you have? Nickels? Dimes? Quarters?

73¢

Using pennies, nickels, dimes, and quarters, players see if they can force the other player to add the last coin to the total on the paper plate to make "exactly" 73¢. The player who adds the last coin loses the game.

Money

Grade 3
Grade 4
Grade 5

Two players

Materials

- paper plate

- tub of pennies, nickels, dimes, and quarters

> This is one of my very favorite games. Children love it and get lots of experience counting and totaling coin amounts. This is also a game of strategy. The more they play, the better children become at thinking ahead and making plans for what they intend to do next.

How to play

The paper plate (the "board") is placed between the two players. Player 1 chooses a coin, places it on the paper plate, and states the value of the coin. Player 2 chooses a coin and places it on the plate. Player 2 must total the two coins and state how much money is now there.

Example

Player 1 puts a dime on the paper plate and says, "The total on the board is ten cents." Player 2 puts a nickel on the plate and says, "There is now fifteen cents on the board."

Players alternate turns, adding one coin at a time and totaling the amount of money on the board. The winner is the player who forces the other player to add the last coin to total exactly 73¢.

> When children first begin to play this game, some of them may take considerable time and effort to count the value of the coins on the paper plate each time. This is completely normal. The more often children do it, the better they will become at this task.

Questions

- Have you discovered any helpful strategies?

- What will you do differently the next time you play the game?

- How did you figure out how much is on the board?

- There is 63¢ on the board. What coins could you safely add to the board? Why?

Variation 1: The game is played in exactly the same manner, but the player who adds the last coin to total exactly 73¢ wins.

Variation 2: The game is played to different money amounts, for instance, $1.23.

How Much More to $1.00?

The goal of this game is to have four counters in a vertical, horizontal, or diagonal row.

Money

Grade 3
Grade 4
Grade 5

Two players

Materials

- different counters for each player
- two dice
- "How Much More to $1.00?" game board

39¢	38¢	37¢	36¢	35¢	34¢
49¢	48¢	47¢	46¢	45¢	44¢
59¢	58¢	57¢	56¢	55¢	54¢
69¢	68¢	67¢	66¢	65¢	64¢
79¢	78¢	77¢	76¢	75¢	74¢
89¢	88¢	87¢	86¢	85¢	84¢

How to play

Player 1 rolls the dice and chooses which number to use for dimes and which for pennies. After making her value, she must figure out how much more money is needed to make $1.00, and then put a counter on that amount on the board.

Example

Player 1 rolls a 6 and a 4. She can make either 64¢ or 46¢. Player 1 makes 64¢. She figures out how much more money is needed to make $1.00, and puts a counter on the 36¢ on the board.

Player 2 rolls the dice and proceeds in the same manner.

Play continues until one player has four counters in a vertical, horizontal, or diagonal row.

Some children might find it helpful to use coins when they play this game until they familiarize themselves with it and become more comfortable working with money values and making change.

Questions

- How did you figure out the difference between the value you created and $1.00?
- What was easy about this game? Difficult?

$2.00

The goal of the game is to collect enough coins in five turns to get as close to $2.00 as possible. Players must complete five turns no matter how close they might be to $2.00. This not an "exact" game so the accumulated value can be more than $2.00.

Money

Grade 3
Grade 4
Grade 5

Two players

Materials

- two dice
- tub of pennies, nickels, dimes, and quarters
- "$2.00" game board for each player

Turn	Coins	Total Value
1		
2		
	Accumulated value	
3		
	Accumulated value	
4		
	Accumulated value	
5		
	Accumulated Value	

How to play

The dice are used to determine the number of coins a player can take from the tub on that turn. After the dice are rolled, the number on each indicates a specific quantity of any one coin denomination a player may take from the tub. A player can choose to pick the same type of coin for each number.

Example

Player 1 rolls a 2 and a 4. He can take two of any one coin and four of any one coin. He may choose to take the same type of coin for both numbers. For example, he takes two nickels; then four nickels.

Player 1 rolls the dice and takes the number of coins indicated by the dice. Player 1 puts her coins on the line for turn 1. She counts the money and consolidates the value of her coins to the fewest number of coins possible.

Example

Player 1 rolls a 2 and a 4. She takes two nickels and four dimes, trades the two nickels for a dime, and then trades all five dimes for two quarters.

Player 1 then records the value in the Total Value column. Player 2 checks Player 1's addition for accuracy. Player 2 rolls the two dice and play proceeds in the same manner.

Players alternate turns until each player has had five turns. The player with the accumulated value closer to $2.00 wins the game.

Example

Player 1's total after five turns is $1.96. Player 2's total after five turns is $2.02. Player 2 is closer to $2.00 and wins the game.

Questions

- What did you discover while playing this game?

- Will you do anything differently the next time you play this game?

- After playing this game several times, did you discover a strategy that was helpful in getting you close to $2.00? What was it?

- How far from $2.00 are you? How did you figure it out?

$5.00

The goal of the game is to be the first player to trade in five $1.00 bills for one $5.00 bill.

Money

Grade 3
Grade 4
Grade 5

Two players

Materials

- tub of coins
- ten $1.00 bills
- one $5.00 bill
- ten-frame cards 1-6, four of each; the same if using a standard deck
- "$5.00" action chart

Draw	Take
1	a penny
2	a nickel
3	a dime
4	three nickels
5	a quarter
6	a $1.00 bill

more4U

How to play

The cards are shuffled and stacked facedown. Player 1 draws two cards and takes the listed number of coins or a $1.00 bill. He must then—

- make all possible trades;
- verbalize the value of his coins; and
- place the cards in a discard pile.

Example

Player 1 draws a 3 and a 4, and takes one dime and three nickels. He trades two of the nickels for a dime, and then trades the two dimes and one nickel for a quarter. He says, "I have one quarter, which is worth twenty-five cents." He places his cards in the discard pile.

Player 2 draws two cards and proceeds in the same manner. (When the cards in the facedown stack have all been used, the cards in the discard pile are shuffled and stacked facedown, and play continues.)

Players alternate turns. The winner is the first player to trade in five $1.00 bills for a $5.00 bill.

Questions

- What was the most difficult part of this game?

- What's the difference between your total and the other player's total?

- How far from $5.00 are you? What did you do to figure it out?

$1,000,000

The goal is to be as close to $1,000,000 as possible after three rounds. This is not an "exact" game, so the total can be more than one million.

Money

Grade 3
Grade 4
Grade 5

Two or more players

Materials

- ten-frame cards with 10s removed, or standard deck with 10s and face cards removed

- paper

- pencils

- "$1,000,000" recording sheet for each player

Round	$100,000	$10,000	$1,000	$100	$10	$1	Total Value
1							
2							
3							
Total							

How to play

The cards are shuffled and stacked facedown. Player 1 draws the first card and places it faceup. The players write this number in any column they choose on the round 1 line of their recording sheet. Players must write this number down immediately. **Once it is written down, it may not be moved to another column.**

Player 2 draws the second card and players write this number in any of the five remaining columns on the round 1 line. Players continue to alternate taking cards until six cards have been drawn and those numbers recorded on the round 1 line.

Players calculate the values for each column, and then write the dollar value for round 1 in the Total Value column.

Example

For the first round, the cards 9, 5, 3, 6, 8, and 2 were drawn. Player 1 wrote them on his recording sheet as follows:

Round	$100,000	$10,000	$1,000	$100	$10	$1	Total Value
1	3 ($300,000)	9 ($90,000)	6 ($6,000)	5 ($500)	8 ($80)	2 ($2)	$396,582

Rounds 2 and 3 are played in the same way.

After three rounds, each player adds their total values for each round for a grand total. The player whose grand total is closest to $1,000,000 wins.

Questions

• How close to $1,000,000 are you? How did you figure it out?

• The next time you play this game, will you do anything differently? Why or why not?

• Have you discovered a strategy that helps you get as close to $1,000,000 as possible?

Integers

Introduction

Comparing Integers

Whose Integer Is Greater?. 255

Money Integers. 256

Adding Integers

Integer Addition 255

Add-It Integers 258

More Integer Addition 259

Salute Integer Addition. 261

Positively Negative 262

Multiplying Integers

Integer Multiplication 264

Introduction

What are integers? Integers are formally defined as positive and negative whole numbers. The whole numbers to the right of 0 on the number line—1, 2, 3, 4, 5, ... and so on—are *positive numbers*. Up until now, this book has printed these numbers without a positive sign, but for this chapter, the negative and positive signs will be used; for instance, the positive number 5 appears as +5.

−5	−4	−3	−2	−1	0	+1	+2	+3	+4	+5

Every positive whole number has an opposite on the other side of the number line to the left of 0. These are the whole *negative numbers*. Every negative number is indicated with a negative sign, so negative 5 is written as −5. Zero is neither positive nor negative.

Two integers are *opposites* if they are each the same distance from zero on opposite sides of the number line. One will have a positive sign, the other a negative sign. The numbers are infinite in both directions.

In our daily lives we use negative numbers to represent quantities such as losses, temperatures below zero, debts, or altitudes below sea level.

The following integer games are the only games in this book that require a standard deck of playing cards with face cards removed. For these games, red cards (diamonds and hearts) are negative numbers; black cards (spades and clubs) are positive numbers.

> If children are new at working with integers, a number line such as the one below might be helpful. You can download it for printing by visiting NCTM's online resources at www.nctm.org/more4u.

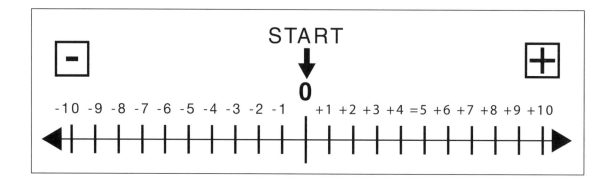

Whose Integer Is Greater?

In this game, children compare their integers and look for the greater number.

Comparing integers
Variation 1: Comparing integers
Variation 2: Adding Integers

Grade 4
Grade 5

Two players

Materials

- standard deck of cards with face cards removed

How to play

Red cards are negative numbers; black cards are positive numbers. The cards are shuffled and dealt facedown between the players. (Players take turns being the dealer.) Players stack their cards facedown.

Players turn over their top card at the same time. Players verbalize their integers to each other. The player with the greater number takes both cards.

Example

Player 1 draws a 5 of hearts and says, "I have a negative five." Player 2 draws a 3 of spades and says, "I have a positive three." Player 2 takes both cards.

In the event of a tie, players turn over another card and put it on top of their first card. The player with the greater number takes all four cards.

Play continues until the facedown cards have all been used. Players count their accumulated cards, and the player with more cards wins the game.

Questions

- How did you decide which player had the greater number?

- Prove to me that +5 is greater than –7.

Variation 1: The game is played the same way, but the player with the lesser integer takes the cards.

Variation 2: "Integer Addition" is played in a similar manner, but each player turns over two cards and adds the integers together. The player with the greater integer sum takes all the cards.

Money Integers

The goal of the game is to have the greater value in coins by the end of the game.

Integers
Money

Grade 4
Grade 5

Two players

Materials

- tub of pennies, nickels, dimes, and quarters
- standard deck of cards with face cards removed

How to play

Each player starts the game with 50¢ in coins from the "bank" (tub):

- three dimes
- three nickels
- five pennies

If a player draws a black number (positive integer) from the deck, the player takes that value in coins from the bank. If a player draws a red number (negative integer) from the deck, the player pays that value in coins to the bank.

The cards are shuffled and stacked facedown. Player 1 draws a card and proceeds according to the rules of play. He places the card in a discard pile. Player 2 draws a card and proceeds in the same manner.

Example

Player 1 turns over a red 8 (negative 8) and takes 8¢ of his money and gives it to the bank. Player 2 then draws a black 10 (positive 10) and takes 10¢ from the bank and adds it to her money.

If a player "goes broke," that player loses his turns until he draws a positive number and can take money from the bank.

Players alternate turns until all the cards in the facedown stack have been used. Players then add up the value of their coins; the player whose coins have the greater value wins the game.

Questions

- What was easy about this game? More difficult?

- What did you do when you needed to give the bank 8¢ but you didn't have a nickel and three pennies?

- How did you figure it out?

Variation: The game is played in exactly the same way, but before the game begins, players make an estimate as to how much money they will have when the game is over. Each player writes his or her estimate down. At the end of the game, the player whose value is closer to his estimate is the winner.

- How close was your estimate to your actual final amount?

Integers

257

Add-It Integers

The goal of this game is to add two integers and get the correct sum.

Adding integers

Grade 4

Grade 5

Two players

Materials

- standard deck of cards with face cards removed

- paper

- pencils

How to play

Red cards are negative numbers; black cards are positive numbers. The cards are shuffled and dealt facedown between the players. (Players take turns being the dealer.) Players stack their cards facedown.

Each player turns over the top card at the same time. Players add these two numbers, write down the equation, and read their equations to each other. If a player's sum is correct, the player gets a point. The two cards are placed in a discard pile. Players turn over their next card and the play proceeds in the same manner.

Example

Player 1 turns over a red 8. Player 2 turns over a black 3.

−8 + +3 = −5. Players write down their equations and read them to each other. Players who have negative 5 as the answer get one point..

When all the facedown cards have been used, players count their points. The player with more points wins.

Questions

- What did you do to figure out the sum of these two numbers?

- What was easy about this game? More difficult?

- What have you discovered about integers while playing this game?

Variation: The game is played the same way but without paper and pencils. Both players turn over their top cards and mentally add the two integers. The first player to say the correct sum out loud takes both cards. In the event of a tie, both players turn over their next card and put it on top of their first card. The first player to verbalize the correct sum of the two new cards collects all four cards.

More Integer Addition

The goal of this game is to have the greater sum when adding two integers.

Adding integers
Variation: Adding integers with three addends

Grade 4
Grade 5

Two players

Materials

- standard deck of cards with face cards removed

- paper

- pencils

How to play

Red cards are negative numbers; black cards are positive numbers. The cards are shuffled and dealt facedown between the players. (Players take turns being the dealer.) Players stack their cards facedown.

Players turn over their top two cards, add the two numbers, write down the equation, and read their equations to each other. The player with the greater sum collects the four cards.

> You may have to explain to the children that when both players have negative sums, the one closer to 0 is greater. This is when the negative and positive number line on page 254 can be helpful.

Example

Player 1 turns over a red 5 and a red 2, both negative integers.

$-5 + -2 = -7$

Player 2 turns over a black 6 and a red 4, one positive and one negative integer.

$+6 + -4 = +2$

Player 2 takes all four cards.

In the event of a tie, players take two more cards, place them on top of their first two cards, and then add the two new numbers together. The player whose integers have the greater sum takes all eight cards.

When the facedown cards have all been used, players count their cards. The player with more cards wins the game.

Questions

- Prove to me that your sum is greater than the other player's sum.

- What did you do to help yourself figure out the sum?

- What have you discovered about integers while playing this game?

- Why is –7 less than +4?

- What was difficult about playing this game? What was easy?

Variation 1: The game is played in the same way but without paper and pencils. Players turn over their top two cards and mentally add the two integers. Players verbalize their equations to each other. The player whose equation has the larger sum takes all four cards. In the event of a tie, both players turn over their next two cards and put them on top of their first ones. As before, players mentally add the two new integers and verbalize their equations to each other. The player whose equation has the larger sum takes all eight cards.

Variation 2: The game is played in a similar way, but players turn over three cards and add up the integers for the greater sum.

Salute Integer Addition

The goal of this game is to figure out the missing addend.

Adding integers with a missing addend

Grade 4
Grade 5

Two players

Materials

- standard deck of cards with face cards removed

How to play

The cards are shuffled and stacked facedown. Red cards are negative numbers; black cards are positive numbers.

Player 1 turns over the top card and places it faceup. He verbalizes the number. Player 2 turns over the next card. She does not look at it, and holds the card to her forehead so only Player 1 can see the second number.

Player 1 mentally adds the two numbers and says the sum out loud. Player 2 mentally calculates what her card must be and says that number out loud. Player 1 decides if Player 2's response is correct. If it is, Player 2 gets one point.

If Player 2 is not correct, she must continue to figure out the number of the card on her forehead; however, she will not get a point.

Example

Player 1 turns over a black 6 and says, "Positive six." Player 2 turns over a red 4 (negative 4), and without looking at it, places it on her forehead. Player 1 says, "My positive six plus the number on your forehead equals positive two." Player 2 mentally calculates what number must be on her forehead. She says, "The number on my forehead is a negative four because positive six plus negative four equals positive two."

Players reverse roles, and play continues until one player has accumulated ten points to win the game.

Questions

- How did you figure out what number card was on your head?
- Convince me that equation is correct.

Positively Negative

Players set up an addition equation with the goal of having the greater sum after adding the two integers together.

Adding integers

Grade 4

Grade 5

Two players

Materials

- die
- two counters for each player
- paper
- pencils
- "Positively Negative" game board for each player

Row 1	8	−5	12	4	−14	2
Row 2	6	−8	−10	−1	6	−3
Row 3	14	1	−15	−9	16	−7
Row 4	−2	11	20	7	5	0
Row 5	−16	−6	3	−12	18	−20
Row 6	9	0	15	−17	−4	−11

How to play

Player 1 rolls the die; the number rolled indicates from which row she must select a number. She puts a counter on any number she chooses in that row.

Example

Player 1 rolls a 3. She puts one of her counters on the number she has selected in Row 3.

Player 2 rolls the die and proceeds in the same manner.

Player 1 rolls the die a second time. If she put her first counter on a positive number, she must put her remaining counter on a negative number in the indicated row or vice versa. If a player rolls the same number for both turns, then the two numbers must be selected from that row.

Player 2 rolls the die a second time and proceeds in the same manner.

Using the selected numbers, each player now writes down an addition equation that will have the greatest sum possible. Players should check each other's computations for accuracy. The player with the greater sum is the winner of that round and earns one point. The first player to earn ten points wins the game.

Questions

- Did you have a reason for putting your counters where you did?
- Have you discovered a strategy for getting the greater sum?
- Prove to the other player that you have the greater sum.
- Why was your sum greater?
- Why is _____ a greater sum than _____?

Integer Multiplication

The goal of this game is to have the greater product after multiplying two integers together.

Multiplying integers

Grade 4

Grade 5

Two players

Materials

- standard deck of cards with face cards removed

- paper

- pencils

How to play

Red cards are negative numbers; black cards are positive numbers.

Discuss the rules for integer multiplication with the children:

- The product of a positive integer and a negative integer is a negative integer.

- The product of two negative integers or two positive integers is a positive integer.

The cards are shuffled and dealt facedown between the players. (The players take turns being the dealer.) Players stack their cards facedown.

They turn over their top card; they write down the equation, and multiply the two numbers. The first player to say the correct product out loud takes both cards. If there is a tie, players turn over the next card on their stacks and multiply the new numbers together. The first player to verbalize the correct product takes all four cards.

Example

Player 1 turns over a red 4; Player 2 turns over a red 6. They write down their equations:

$-4 \times -6 = +24$ *or*

$-6 \times -4 = +24$

Player 2 says, "Positive twenty-four!" before Player 1. He takes the two cards.

Play continues until all the facedown cards have been used. Players count their accumulated cards; the one with more cards wins the game.

Questions

- What was easy for you when playing this game? What was more difficult?
- Convince me that _____ x _____ equals _____.

<u>Variation:</u> The game is played the same way but without paper and pencils. Both players turn over their top cards and mentally multiply the two integers. The first player to verbalize the correct product takes both cards. In the event of a tie, both players turn over their next card and multiply the new numbers. The first player to verbalize the correct product of the two new cards collects all four cards.

References

Duncan, Greg J., and Amy Claessens. "School Readiness and Later Achievement." *Journal of Developmental Psychology* 43, no. 6 (November 2007): 1428–1446.

Kaye, Peggy. *Games for Math: Playful Ways to Help Your Child Learn Math, from Kindergarten to Third Grade.* New York: Pantheon Books, 1988.

National Council of Teachers of Mathematics (NCTM). *Math, Fun, and Games?: Yes Way!* Reston, Va.: NCTM, n.d. http://www.nctm.org/resources/content.aspx?id=27612.

——. *Principals and Standards for School Mathematics.* Reston, Va.: NCTM, 2000.

National Governors Association Center for Best Practices (NGA Center) and Council of Chief State School Officers (CCSSO). *Common Core State Standards for Mathematics. Common Core State Standards (College- and Career-Readiness Standards and K–12 Standards in English Language Arts and Math).* Washington, D.C.: NGA Center and CCSSO, 2010. http://www.corestandards.org.

National Parent Teacher Association (PTA). *Parents' Guide to Student Success: 3rd Grade.* Alexandria, Va.: National PTA, 2011. http://www.pta.org/files/3rd%20Grade%20June20.pdf.

——. *Parents' Guide to Student Success: 4th Grade.* Alexandria, Va.: National PTA, 2011. http://www.pta.org/files/4th%20Grade%20June20.pdf.

——. *Parents' Guide to Student Success: 5th Grade.* Alexandria, Va.: National PTA, 2011. http://www.pta.org/files/5th%20Grade%20June20.pdf.

——. *Guía Para Padres Para Fomentar El Éxito Escolar: 3er Grado.* Alexandria, Va.: National PTA, 2011. http://www.pta.org/files/3rd_Grade_spanish_HR_June30.pdf.

——. *Guía Para Padres Para Fomentar El Éxito Escolar: 4to Grado.* Alexandria, Va.: National PTA, 2011. http://www.pta.org/files/4th_Grade_spanish_HR_June30.pdf.

——. *Guía Para Padres Para Fomentar El Éxito Escolar: 5to Grado.* Alexandria, Va.: National PTA, 2011. http://www.pta.org/files/5th_Grade_spanish_HR_June30.pdf.